Plays for You...

Methuen Drama's *Plays for Yo...*
excellent selection of single plays a
people to perform. The series featu
established playwrights, which is age-appropriate and organised
into age bands to help teachers and youth theatre leaders select the
most suitable work for their group.

The Storyteller Sequence

Karamazoo
Fairytaleheart
Sparkleshark
Moonfleece
Brokenville

PHILIP RIDLEY

Bloomsbury Methuen Drama
An imprint of Bloomsbury Publishing Plc

B L O O M S B U R Y
LONDON • NEW DELHI • NEW YORK • SYDNEY

Bloomsbury Methuen Drama
An imprint of Bloomsbury Publishing Plc

· 50 Bedford Square   1385 Broadway
London   New York
WC1B 3DP   NY 10018
UK   USA

www.bloomsbury.com

Bloomsbury is a registered trade mark of Bloomsbury Publishing Plc

British Library Cataloguing-in-Publication Data
A catalogue record for this book is available from the British Library.

ISBN: PB: 978-1-4742-1699-9
ePub: 978-1-4742-1701-9
ePDF: 978-1-4742-1700-2

Library of Congress Cataloging-in-Publication Data
A catalog record for this book is available from the Library of Congress.

Typeset by Fakenham Prepress Solutions, Fakenham, Norfolk NR21 8NN
Printed and bound in India

THE STORYTELLER SEQUENCE

If you put me and a chimpanzee on an island together
and we had to struggle for survival,
I would place my bets on the chimpanzee.
But if you put a thousand humans
and a thousand chimpanzees on an island
then the humans would clearly win.
Because humans can co-operate much better
and this is because of the stories they tell one another.
Whether the stories are true or not doesn't really matter.

Yuval Noah Harari

Contents

Karamazoo

Female Ace Version

I felt the need to tell stories
to understand myself

Manuel Puig

Characters

Ace

Ace, *fifteen years old, has a hair style and outfit that yell, 'Look at me! I'm gorgeous!' She is speaking into a mobile phone –*

Ace Guess who? Why, it's me. Guess where I am? Oh! Surprise, surprise! I'm at the place where we arranged to meet. Guess who's not here? Guess who's hacking me off? Guess whose life won't be worth living if he don't turn up here in the next sixty seconds. Bye!

Hangs up.

This is what happens when you make a date with a bloody Hatchling – Oh! That's one of *my* words. It describes a certain kind of boy. One who acts like a baby duck. You know? After a duck pecks out its shell the first thing it claps eyes on – Quack-quack! Love! Well, that's what Mr Not Here On Time was like. First day I joined the school – There he is! Eyes wide. Tongue down to his knees. Pure Hatchling! I've got words for most sorts of people. I'm good with words. I take after my Dad but … well, that's another story.

Slight pause.

Charity! That's what my agreeing to meet him is. He's not even cute. A Hatchling can sometimes be amusing if they're cute. Nicole – she had a Hatchling last year by all accounts, and she says he used to buy her little presents and send her love poems and – more importantly – looked terrific without his shirt on. I've seen a photo of him and, believe me, that boy put the 'it' back in fit. A Hatchling like that I could live with. A Hatchling like that I might even encourage. But my one – and I don't wanna sound mean, I really don't, but facts is facts and he puts the 'ug' back in ugly. He wears T-shirts the size of marquees for one thing which is usually a sign of acute six-pack shortage in my experience. And as for his ears…well, let's just say if a strong wind catches him unawares he could end up in Alaska quicker than you can say flying elephants. Oh, I know what you're thinking. Bitchy cow. But I'm not. I'm just being honest. Nicole understands. Nicole and me have got what you'd call 'like minds'. I like her's and she likes mine. Me and her go way, way back. We met at *Narcissus 'R' Us*. You know? The hairdressers down the market. Well, I say 'hairdressers' but it's more your total beauty salon. Sunbed. Waxing. Facials. And – since last month – nails. I'm saving up to have little hearts painted on each of mine. So far I've got enough for three fingers. Or five toes. The front of the shop has been painted to look like a Greek Temple. Vases. Flowers. Girls in togas. It's all very classy. Admittedly, the effect is slightly diminished by having Mr Cuttymeat's Butchers right next door but once you're inside … oh, it's pure heaven. Really. They play all this floaty music and you just lay back and get told how gorgeous you are. All the girls go there. The *real* girls. The ones that matter … What was I saying? Oh! Meeting Nicole! I went to *Narcissus 'R' Us* one morning to have my eyelashes tinted and a bit of the dye got under my eyelid and – ooo, it did bloody hurt – Nicole rushes over and says, 'Don't rub it, girl. You'll only make it worse. Breathe deep. Let your tears wash it away.' Oh, she was terrific. Really. She held my hand through the whole thing. Well, that was it! Someone helps you through a trauma like that you're friends for life. I saw this documentary about an earthquake once. They had an interview with this woman. I forget her name but her make-up was a mess. Anyway, she was talking about her earthquake experience. Trapped in her car, she was. Her legs were crushed. Flat as burgers from the knees down. Blood everywhere. And this total stranger comes up to Messy Make-Up Woman and holds her hand and talks to her and keeps her spirits up while the fireman or whoever cut her free. Minus the legs. And I think, That's like me and Nicole when I got eyelash tint in my eye. Nicole – she couldn't wait for me to start going to her school. We used to count the days. And before you say anything, no, we are *not* a couple of secret lumberjack bush munchers, we're *best friends*. Sisters. I have no inclination to get intimate with a girl no matter how much Bobby Bolter wants to see it.

Dials on phone.

I'm getting wound up now. You offer a Hatchling with deformed ears and a flaccid stomach a date out of the goodness of your heart and – (*into phone*) Guess who? Me again! Guess what I'm doing? Still waiting for you! Listen! I'm gonna put this as delicately as I can. If you are not here within the next sixty seconds, Ugly Person, I will do everything in my power to emotionally cripple you for the rest of your life. Bye, Jamie!

Hangs up.

That's his name. Jamie.

Slight pause.

I'm Ace, by the way. Nickname. 'Cos I am. Ace body. Ace hair.
Ace teeth. Need I carry on? I was gonna have it tattooed – Here.
At the bottom of my spine. But then I saw a lifetime of boys
wise-cracking about ace in the hole so I decided against it. I'm
determined to have a tattoo done somewhere, though. Nicole said
I should get my tongue pierced like hers. No thank you! I went
with her when she had it done and it was, without doubt, the
most horrific thing I have ever witnessed, second only to what I
saw Micky Wignall doing with half a melon in his back garden
when we were twelve and if you press me on that I'll scream, I
swear I will. Miss Kizzie B – that's the person in charge of body
ornamentation at *Narcissus 'R' Us* – grabbed Nicole's tongue
between her finger and thumb and pulled it out so far I half
expected to see Nic's kidneys on the other end and then – those
with a weak stomach should plug their ears now – Miss Kizzie
B nail-gunned – I repeat: *nail gunned* – this stud right through
it. Bahm! Miss Kizzie B said, 'There! That didn't hurt, did it?'
Nicole was screaming too much to answer. And her tongue was
already swelling up. And turning blue. If you didn't know better
you'd swear she was in a Who Can Put The Largest Aubergine
In Their Mouth Competition. And if you meet Monica and she
tells you I rushed to the toilets to throw up that is *not* the case.
I'd eaten a suspect fillet o' fish and it had gone right through me,
that's all. Honestly, Monica can be such a bloody Commercial
sometimes – Commercial! That's another one of my words. When
you can't believe a word anyone says. You know? Oh, there's lots
of words I could apply to Monica. None of them what you'd call
complimentary. She's got a pleasant enough face I grant you – if
you like that sort of thing – but she's the kind of girl who can
spend all day getting herself ready for a night out and still turn up
looking like she's just survived a tsunami. And please don't think
I'm being two faced because that is not my style. I am not saying
anything to you that I have not said to Monica's face.

Slight pause.

Life's so much easier when you've whacked a label on someone, don't you think? Of course, people can have more than one label. Jamie, for example, is a Hatchling and a Supermarket Neon. That's ugly but bright. Monica – and, again, I'll give you just two otherwise, with her, we'll be here for hours – she is a Commercial and a Lava Lamp. Laver Lamp? That's pretty to look at but not too bright. Good, eh? I could be on telly I reckon. The best thing to be labelled, needless to say, is a Summer Sunrise. Totally bright and totally gorgeous. There's only two Summer Sunrises in our school. Me and Nicole. Although, truth told, I've got a few more sunbeams than her. Don't get me wrong. Nicole's as Olympic as they come. Totally fit. When she gets up on the dance floor and does that butt-thrusty, lip-pouty, tit-pointy thing of her's … well, I've seen grown men faint – thump! – right before my eyes. It's just with Nicole … oh, how can I put this without sounding unkind? … Nicole's dress sense can sometimes be … misguided. Take the night of Monica's fifteenth birthday party. Nicole had got it into her head she wanted to get a Helen of Troy. That's this all over bronzing treatment they do down at 'Narcissus 'R' Us'. They sort of spray paint the tan on you. Like they paint cars. Cost Nicole a mini fortune. Then Nicole decides she's gonna wear these yellow hot pants. And this short sleeved T-shirt. Now, of course, there *is* a way this outfit could've worked – if *I'd* worn it, for example – but the trouble was Nicole's tan…well, it had not quite come out as … 'au naturel' as she'd been led to expect. Not so much bronze as … oh, what's the word? Formica! And, what made it worse, Nicole's legs and arms are not as … substantial as they should me. Well, after a three year diet of laxatives and *Hula Hoops* what d'you expect. I tell you, when I saw her that night – oh, I don't like to say this. She's my friend. My sister – but it was like Pinocchio in drag, I swear it was.

Slight pause.

Sausages 'n' Custard! I've got to tell you about them. A Sausages 'n' Custard is someone's who's just a total and utter mistake. Just the sight of them – like looking at sausages and custard – makes you puke. There's a few Sausages 'n' Custards at school but the worst is, without doubt, Ruth. Oh, where do I start with Ruth? She a fat cow. And as everyone knows – even the dimmest of Lava Lamps – thighs the size of tugboats can never be forgiven, no matter what other good points a person might have. In Ruth's case, however, there are no good points. Honestly, I've seen road kill with more sexual allure. There's few people in this world that I truly hate – because I have a naturally caring and forgiving nature and I refuse to pollute my karma with negative emotions – but I do hate Ruth. I just don't see the point to people who are not pleasing to the eye. There should be a law against it or something. If I wasn't a Summer Sunrise – which I quite clearly am – I'd kill myself.

Slight pause.

I was browsing round Shoezie For The Choozie the other day – oh, that shop is class. I buy all my foot ware there. Most girls do. The *real* girls. You can't actually walk properly in any of their shoes, of course, not without breaking a few minor bones and getting blisters the size of muffins but – hey! – beauty knows no pain, eh? Anyway, who strolls into the shop casual as you like but Ruth! There's no one else around so I give her a quick smile and a nod the way you do. She asks how I am. I say, 'Totally gorgeous, thank you. And how are *you*?' Which is a bit like asking the Elephant Man what he thinks of lip gloss but you don't want to be rude, do you. Ruth asks, 'How's your Mum coping?' I say, 'Very well, thank you.' Then she asks, 'And how're *you* coping?' I say, 'Fine.' She says, 'Are you *sure*?' And I can see where Ruth's heading with this – all that '*I* know you better than *you* know you' psychobabble – so I say, 'You've gotta wise up, Ruth! Look at your hair! Your clothes! Your nails! Honestly, girl, you might not be no oil painting but even a tacky photocopy can be put in a decent frame. And, while we're on the subject, read my top lip! Female moustache. Get waxing, girl!' She starts crying, of course. Ruth's always been a Niagara Falls in the waterworks department. Has no effect on me. I'm a Duck's Back where tears are concerned. Especially Ruth's. I've made her cry lots of times in the past. I'll do it lots of times in the future probably. Definitely! Why not? She asks for it!

Dials on phone.

Okay. Just to show you I'm not the cold hearted bitch you all
think I am because I can tell what's on your mind, don't deny it
… (*into phone*) Guess who? I was just thinking…perhaps you've
forgotten where we're meeting. It's that old shelter by the library.
I'm only gonna be here for another minute and then I'm off so get
a move on. If not – you're toast!

Hangs up.

I said I'd meet him here cos no one from school goes anywhere
near the library. Only the geeks. And they don't count. Mum
and Dad used to meet here. When they were both my age.
Somewhere in all this graffiti there's their names in a heart.
So Mum says. I've never seen it. …There's 'Kyra 4 Tony' and
'Susan Loves Stevo' and 'Roman and Kelsey Forever'. So
many. Some of these dates go back years and years. Before I
was born. A lifetime of people loving each other forever and
ever. Stupid sods. There is no forever. It's crap. All of it! *I*
know!

Phone rings.

At last! – Oh, it's Nicole … (*into phone*) Hi, girlfriend, what's
the story?…No, no, I'm on my way to *Narcissus* to get ask Miss
Kizzy about – …Nah, nah, Nic, don't bother, by the time you get
there I'll be – … Oh, are you? … Yeah, yeah, but … Okay, Nic,
you've caught me out. I'm being a bit of a Commercial. I'm not
going to *Narcissus* – Hang on, girl! Don't blow a bloody fuse! I'm
on me way to the cemetery … Yeah, I know, but it's coming up to
the first anniversary next month so I thought – … I'll be fine, Nic.
Yeah. I promise. See you later.

Hangs up.

I'm not proud of that. Lying to a fellow Summer Sunrise goes
against all my principals. And I am not proud of bringing
Dad's death into it either. But I had to keep Nicole off the scent
somehow. Can you imagine what she'd've thought if she knew
who I was waiting to – Oh, I don't even wanna think about it. My

credibility would have plummeted faster than Monica's knickers in the boy's toilets.

Slight pause.

She came with me once. Nicole. To the cemetery. About a month ago. I thought I was gonna be just fine. Cleaned the little vase and put some lillies in it. Dad loved lillies. Nicole said how one of the stone angels needed to lose a few pounds around the waist and we had a giggle. And then ... then I see this man walking down the path. And there's something about the tilt of his head. Or maybe it's his hair. But he looks like Dad and, for a split second, I'm about to call out, 'Dad!' Well, that starts it off. Niagara Falls with a vengeance, wasn't I. Oh, it was so humiliating. Really. Nicole says, 'Get a grip, girl!' and then – whooooshh! She's instant Mascara. When things get emotional – she runs! I don't blame her. I'd done the same in her shoes. Not that I'd ever wear shoes like Nicole. Nicole and me never talk about Dad now. If he pops into the conversation – accidental like – Nicole changes the subject.

Looks at phone.

Slight pause.

It's where I met him. Jamie. In the cemetery. Well, it's where I *talked* to him for the first time. Couple of weeks ago. I was walking through the gate and I heard this voice go, 'Hello, Ace.' We walked down the path together. He's got blue eyes. I ask him who he's got buried there and he says, 'No one. I come here to do some thinking.' And I say, 'I can think of better places.' And he says, 'Well, if people didn't keep picking on me everywhere I go *I* could think of better places too!' We sit on this wooden seat. He asks when my Dad died and I say, 'Last August. August the seventh.' And he asks what of and I say, 'Cancer.' And he says it must have been awful and, suddenly, it's like something bursts in my throat and I'm telling him all these things about Dad, the second hand shop where Dad used to work and how he used to love old photographs of people he never knew and how people used to go there just to tell Dad their problems cos Dad could talk to anyone, just anyone, and ... and how Dad used to tell me stories to help me get to sleep ... wonderful stories ...

Slight pause.

They weren't from books or anything. The stories Dad told me.
He made them up. Made them up as he went along. I said to
him once, 'You should write them down, Dad, else you'll forget
them.' He said, 'Oh, I'm too busy for that, sweetheart. Why don't
you do it for me?' And I was going to! I bought a notebook and
everything. But … well, you think you've got forever to do things
like that, don't you. Someone's always been there doing certain
things, you can't imagine them not being there doing certain
things. It's like someone saying to you, 'Don't forget to take a
photograph of the sky in case you forget what it looks like.' And
you think, What's the rush? The sky's always gonna be there.

Slight pause.

I've been trying to remember as many as I can now. Dad's stories.

Slight pause.

I told one to Jamie. When we were the cemetery … Once there
was girl – Dad always described the girl so she looked like me.
My hair. My smile. And this girl lived in a hut on the edge of
a forest with her dad. The girl and her dad were so happy. And
then, one day, the Dad became ill – Nothing serious. A chill or
something. But he has to go to bed. The girl makes him some
soup and looks after him and, while he's taking a nap, she leaves
the hut and strolls to the edge of the forest and – A feather. She
picks it up. Then she sees another. She picks that up too. Another.
And she follows this trail of feathers deep into the heart of the
forest. She doesn't mean to go there. It's the feathers leading her
on. And then – Birds! Look at them! They're wonderful! Flying
from branch to branch. Oh, the girl is so happy just looking at
them. And then the girl hears a voice say, 'I'm so thirsty.' And the
girl sees an old man sitting on the grass. The girl gives him some
of her lemonade to drink – Oh! I forgot that bit. The girl has a
bottle of lemonade. Don't ask me how or why. Perhaps she always
goes out with a bottle. I dunno. The girl says, 'Those birds are so
gorgeous! I wish I could be a one of them for a while.' And the old
man says, 'Surprise! I'm a Wizard. I will grant your wish because

you shared your lemonade with me. But be warned … being a
bird is so wonderful you might forget who you really are if you
stay one for too long. I'm going to tell you a magic word that will
change you back into a girl. Only *you* can change yourself back.
No one else can do it for you. To be safe, make sure you say this
magic word as soon as you see the sun begin to set. The word is
… Karamazoo!' You must say it three times. You understand? You
must say Karamazoo three times before the bird form takes you
over forever.' 'I understand,' says the girl. And so the Wizard turns
the girl into – Well, you can guess the rest. She has a great time
as a bird. She sees the sun setting and thinks, I'll say the magic
word in a minute. And one minute becomes two. Then three. Four.
An hour. Until the sky is full of stars. But, by then, it's too late.
Because now the girl has forgotten she has ever been a girl. And
when she hears the sound of a man calling for his daughter … in
the forest … she doesn't even remember who he is ….

Slight pause.

It's not a Niagara Falls or anything. I must still have some
blue-black eyelash tint stuck in my eye somewhere.

Looks at phone.

It's just such a slap in the face. Well, don't you think? He must
have got my messages. He checks his messages every two
minutes. I've see him. His sister's not well. She's in a wheelchair.
She's got that … muscular thing wrong with her. Motor Neuron
whatever. Jamie's always worrying about her.

Slight pause.

I've brought a photo to show him. Of me. A few years ago.

Slight pause.

I'm gonna shock you now. Fasten your safety belts – Once …
I was *not* a Summer Sunrise. I used to go to school – my *old*
school. The one they turned into luxury flats – and I'd sit at the
back of the class and no one used to talk to me except Ruth and
we – … Okay, okay! Another shock! Those with heart problems
should take their medication now. I used to be friends with

Sausages 'n' Custard Ruth. Her dad was best friends with my dad so … what can I say? It was another life! Things change. We have to move on. I've tried to help Ruth. I've offered her advice. It's not my fault she hasn't got what it takes! I can't be responsible for the likes of her. I've got enough problems of my own.

Slight pause.

I could phone Bobby Bolter! He's my male equivalent at school. A *male* Summer Sunrise. Bobby – he'd be here in a flash. He'd sell his grandmother for a date with me.

Slight pause.

You know what really upset me. They knocked it down. The second hand shop where Dad used to work. Just three weeks after he died. Three weeks! They turned it into a pile of rubble. Demolished the whole street.

Slight pause.

I went onto it once. The demolition site. They'd put a fence all round it but … there was a gap.

Slight pause.

I remember … Cold…It was snowing … I have to be careful where I walk … Oh, look! That bit of wall … It's from Dad's shop…I recognise the paint … Dad liked the colour … He said it was cheerful … And I stand there. In the snow and rubble. Just looking at this bit of wall. And I can feel the tears freezing on my face. And I think, I'm gonna change! … I'm gonna be different … I'm not gonna be Invisible anymore. I wanna be like those girls I've seen going into *Narcissus R Us*. I wanna wear the clothes they wear. I wanna walk like them. Talk like them. I'm gonna change! I know what to do! Soon as New Year hit's I'm losing weight. New body! New hair! Facials! Eyelash tint! Hair extensions! New name! New walk! Bury the old me! Bury her deep! Who wants to be a person who stands in rubble with frozen tears on their face? Not me! No way! I'm Ace now. Total sunrise. I don't need any of you. I don't need *anyone*.

Pause.

That's it! I'm not gonna wait here anymore! Time to make other plans.

Dials on phone.

I'm phoning Nicole. He's had his chance! He can rot in hell for all I – (*into phone*) Nicole, what's the story, girl? Course I'm alright. Why shouldn't I be? Where are you? Well, wait there! I'm coming straight over! What you say we go down the club and do some serious posing? You up for that …? Me too!

Hangs up.

I tell you, when me and Nicole strut our stuff … no one can touch us. I've seen other girls look at us and … well, they've been so intimated you can see the will to live just drain out of them.

Phone rings.

Would you believe it, eh? The Prince of Too Late! – (*into phone*) What d'you want, Jamie? … No! No excuses! I'm not waiting at the shelter now anyway. I left ages ago … Park your lips! I don't care if your sister had a fall or if … if she was struck by bloody lightening. This whole thing's a big set up anyway. Nicole was hiding. She was gonna buy me five painted nails down at *Narcissus* if I dared to kiss you. Know why that's such a dare? Cos your breath stinks like something crawled down your throat and died. You stink and you're ugly and you're flabby and –

Slight pause.

He hung up! Some people just can't take criticism. Turned the waterworks on he did too. Strange to hear a boy cry. Why should I care? I'm a Summer Sunrise. Why should I care about someone like him … Who does he think I am …? Who does he think … I am …?

Slight pause.

Karamazoo … Karamazoo … Karamazoo …

Fade to blackout.

Karamazoo

Male Ace Version

*I felt the need to tell stories
to understand myself*

Manuel Puig

Characters

Ace

Ace, *fifteen years old, has both a hair style and outfit that yell,
'Look at me! I'm gorgeous!' He is speaking into a mobile phone –*

Ace What's the story, eh? We said six o'clock. Know what the
time is now? Two minutes past! Told you, I don't wait. Call me
when you get this. You've got one minute. Then I'm off. *Your*
loss.

Hangs up.

Can you believe it? Eh? The bloody nerve! It's *her* that's been
drooling for a date. First day I joined the school she gave me this
… yearning look. Yearning and pleading. Like a puppy when
you're about to thump it one. Not that I've ever thumped a puppy.
Or any animal. Love animals, me. Well, okay, I admit, I *did* put
my terrapin in the microwave when I was seven but that was a
long time ago and if I'd know it was gonna cause that much mess
I wouldn't've done it in the first place. Mum – she was upset. Hit
the roof. But … hey, that's another story.

Slight pause.

Charity. That's what my agreeing to meet her is. I don't wanna
call the girl a dog – cos I'm an old fashioned boy at heart and
I've got manners – but let's just say God was at the bottom of the
beauty bucket when He came to her. Don't get me wrong, I've
got nothing against ugly people. Uggers're fine. In their place.
The way I see it … well, it's like sport! Boxing, say! You do
not put a flyweight no hoper in the ring with a heavy weight at
the top of his form. Same with looks. It is inhumane – I repeat:
in-hum-mane – to put uggers in the same living space as people
like me. You see, I'm what's called an alpha male. Danny thought
that one up. He's good with words, is Danny. Me and him hit it
off – Bahm! – the first time we met. Down the cafe it was. You
know the one? Next to that second hand computer place. Me
and Danny happened to sit at the same table one morning for a
fry up and seven hours later – seven hours! – we were *still* there
– still jabbering away – and knocking back an afternoon Coke
and doughnut like we'd known each other all our lives. Danny
couldn't wait for me to join his school. We used to count the

days to the start of the new term. And before you say anything, no, I was *not* expelled from my last school. They turned it into luxury flats – Where was I? … Alpha males! If we were all jungle creatures – I'd be the lion. Sea creatures – the Great White. Air – eagle. Neat, eh? When I get the money I'm gonna have tattoos done. Lion. Shark. Eagle. Danny's got a tattoo. A crocodile. It starts here and goes all the way down his back. I went with him to have it done. Sweating with the pain, he was. And there was blood. Never occurred to me the thing would bleed. Did it you? Never me. And if you meet Ewan or Dixie and they tell you I fainted tell them that's bollocks! I did *not* faint. I was just so bored I slipped out my bloody seat, that's all.

Dials on phone.

I'm getting wound up now. You offer a dog charity out of the goodness of your bloody heart and – (*into phone*) I hope for your sake you didn't get my last message because if you did and you *still* not making contact then life's gonna be merry hell for you in the playground. I'll give you one more minute. Then I'm off. So wise up, Holly!

Hangs up.

That's her name. Holly.

Slight pause.

I'm Ace, by the way. Nickname. Alpha male? Ace? Get it? – Look! This is the way it works at school. In the boys, there's me and Danny, the two Alpha males, top of the food chain. Although, truth told, Danny's probably just a bit below me. He's sort of Alpha minus whereas I'm Alpha plus. Danny hasn't quite got it in the body department, you see. Now, don't get me wrong, he's not chopped liver and he looks pretty hot without his shirt, especially with that tattoo, and before you say anything, no, I am *not* a secret shirt tail lifter, despite what some people say about me and Danny always being together, it's just that he's the only other alpha male within a radius of twenty miles and everyone knows alphas have to stick together otherwise the whole food chain will fall apart and the result will be chaos, sheer bloody chaos, and I will not have

that on my conscience for you or anyone, thank you very much –
Hang on! Is that Holly coming? … Nah. Not her.

Slight pause.

Food chain. Me and Danny, tippity-top. Under me and Danny are
the Alpha Wannabes. It is not advisable, in my opinion, for Alpha's
to mix with Alpha Wannabes. It is degrading and humiliating for us
both. Alphas can, however, mix with the Worker Ants. The Worker
Ants are your Ewans and Dixies of the world. Worker Ants will
never be Alphas and they know it. They are content to carry bags
and do little errands and be the butt of jokes just so long as they
can bathe in the dazzling radiance that emanates from someone like
me. Now, below the Worker Ants you start getting into the dregs.
If you've got protective clothing put it on now. First, there's the
Invisibles. They're the ones you never notice. You know when the
teacher says, 'Where's Billy Turner? He hasn't been in class all
week.' And you think, Who the bloody hell's Billy Turner? *That's*
an Invisible. And then, below that, you have the lowest of the low.
Geeks! The plankton of the food chain. The biggest geek in our
school is Josh. Blimey, where do I begin with Josh? He's like a …
You know when you burst a zit? And it sort of scabs over. And then
you pick the scab off and you look at it in your hand. And it's all red
and flecked with dry puss. And some time's there's a hair sticking
out of it. Well, put a school uniform on that and you've got Josh.

Slight pause.

I was waiting at the bus stop the other day. The one down by
the bingo hall. You know? And who walks up – Josh the Geek.
There's no one else around so I give him a quick, 'Hello.' Believe
me, I do *not* want to make conversation, but when there's just the
two of you at a bloody bus stop – what can you do? Josh says,
'How's your Dad coping?' I say, 'Fine.' He says, 'And how're
you coping?' I say, 'Fine.' He says, 'Are you *sure*?' And I can see
where Josh is heading with this – all that '*I* know you better than
you know you' psychobabble – so I say, 'You've gotta wise up,
Josh! Look at your hair! Your clothes! Jeez!' He says, 'I'm just
being myself. Which is more than I can say for you.' I thump him
one. Hard. I don't care! I'll make his life hell! I will! I *have*!

Dials on phone.

Okay. Just to show you I'm not the heartless so-and-so you think
I am cos I can tell what you're all thinking, don't deny it, I'm not
stupid … listen to this – (*into phone*) Holly, I was thinking …
perhaps you've forgotten where we're meeting. It's that old shelter
by the library. I'm only gonna be here for one more minute – then
I'm off so get a move on. You've got sixty seconds! Fifty-nine …
fifty-eight … fifty-seven …

Hangs up.

I said I'd meet her here cos no one from school goes anywhere
near the library. Only the geeks. And they don't count – Well,
I've got my reputation to maintain. Usually, I just snap my fingers
and – whoooshh! – girls are at my feet. Pronto! I don't wanna say
they're gagging for it cos I'm not the bragging type but facts is
facts and they are. You know those pictures on the news? When
there's some famine somewhere and the army or whatever goes in
with food and soldiers throw parcels from the backs of lorries and
all these starving people are going, 'Me! Me!' Well, that's what
girls're like at the prospect of snogging yours truly. If you go into
the girl's toilets at school, third cubicle, you'll see, 'Tick here if
you wanna snog Ace'. The wall is black with ticks. All the walls.
Ceiling. There's not enough space in that cubicle for the number
of girls who wanna play tonsil hockey with yours truly. There's
the same question about Danny in the second cubicle. That wall's
half full. Now, don't get me wrong, Danny don't go short in the
girl department. He can get any girl he wants too. He's just on
a slower burn than me. Danny's got the broody thing going for
him. He's the mysterious one. Some girls go for all that. They
like gazing up at the moon and reciting poetry. Stuff like that does
not float my boat in any way, shape or form. When I have a date
you can forget moonlight and sweet words. I want a beer and a
boogie and gums round my plums before midnight. What's wrong
with that? At least I'm honest. I don't lead girls on. I say to them,
'Girls, I'm not promising you the world, I'm just promising you a
glimpse of paradise.'

Phone rings.

About time – Oh, it's Danny … Hey, what's the story, man? …
Nah, I'm in the gym … Nah, nah, mate, don't bother. By the time
you get here I'll be – …Oh, you're just round the corner, are you?
… Yeah, yeah, but … Okay, mate, you've caught me out. I'm not
at the gym. I'm on me way to the cemetery … Yeah, I know, but
it's coming up to a year next month so I thought – … Sure! Phone
you later. Cheers, mate!

Hangs up.

I'm not proud of that. Lying to a mate is a major no-no in my
books. And I'm not proud of bringing the anniversary of Mum's
death into it either. But I had to keep Danny off the scent
somehow. Can you imagine what he'd've thought if he knew who
I was about to meet – Oh, I don't even wanna think about it. I'm
shaking! Look! Jeez!

Slight pause.

He came with me once. Danny. To the cemetery. About a month
ago. I thought I was gonna be okay. Put flowers in the little vase
thing. Danny said how one of the stone angels looked like it was
getting it up the back and we had a laugh. And then … then I see
this woman walking down the path. And there's something about
the tilt of her head. Or maybe it's her hair. But she looks just like
Mum and, for a split second, I'm gonna call out, 'Mum!' Well,
that starts it off. Bloody water works. Embarrassing or what?
Danny looks all awkward and – whoosh! Can't see him for dust.
Don't blame him. Danny and me never talk about Mum now. If
she pops into the conversation – accidental like – Danny changes
the subject pronto.

Looks at phone.

… It's where I met her. Holly. In the cemetery. Well, it's where
I *talked* to her for the first time. Couple of weeks ago. I was
walking through the gate and I heard this voice go, 'Hello, Ace.'
We walked down the path together. She's got blue eyes. I ask her
who she's got buried there and she says, 'No one. I come here to
do some thinking.' And I say, 'I can think of better places,' And
she says, 'Well, if people didn't keep picking on me everywhere I

go *I* could think of better places too!' We sit on this wooden seat.
She asks when Mum died and I say, 'A year ago next month.' And
she asks what of and I say, 'Cancer.' And she says it must have
been awful and, suddenly, it's like something bursts in my throat
and I'm telling her all these things, the launderette where Mum
worked, and how mum made cups of tea and everyone told Mum
all their problems cos Mum could talk to anyone, just anyone, and
how mum told me stories to help me get to sleep at night and the
stories were always so brilliant … brilliant …

Slight pause.

She made them up. The stories. Mum. Made them up as she went
along. I said to her, 'You should write them down, Mum, else
you'll forget.' She said, 'Oh, I'm too busy for that, love. Why
don't you do it for me?' And I was *going* to! Bought a notebook
and everything. But … well, you think you've got forever to do
things like that, don't you. Someone's always been there doing
certain things, you can't imagine them not being there doing
certain things. It's like someone saying to you, 'Don't forget to
take a photograph of the sky in case you forget what it looks like.'
And you think, What're they talking about? The sky's *always*
gonna be there.

Slight pause.

I've been trying to remember as many as I can now. Mum's
stories.

Slight pause.

I told one to Holly. When we were at the cemetery … Imagine a
forest! Trees! Birds. And there – Look! A little wooden hut. Who
lives in the wooden hut? Why, it's a Boy and his Mum. The Boy
helps Mum with all the housework. What a good little boy he
is – Mum did tell this when I was a toddler so the language is a
bit … basic. One day the boy's Mum says, 'I feel like some fish
and chips for dinner.' The Boy says, 'I'll pop down to the lagoon
and catch us some fish fingers.' So off he trots to the lagoon and –
was it a lagoon? Lake? Anyway, whatever it is, he sits by the edge
of it and waits for a nibble on his fishing rod. But then – Hang

on! What's that? Something's splashing in the middle the water! Silver creatures that make squeaking noises. Dolphins! They look brilliant! Brilliant! Hang on! Who's that? It's an Old Woman. She plonks herself down next to the Boy and the two of them have a natter. The Boy shares his sandwiches with the – Did I mention he had sandwiches? Okay. Mum made the Boy some sandwiches and when this witch sits next to him – Bloody hell! The Old Woman's a Witch. Or perhaps that should've come as a surprise later. Don't look at me like that. It's a bloody tricky story. Where was I? Boy. Water – Dolphins! Okay. So the Boy says, 'Those dolphins are having a lot of fun! I wish I could be a dolphin for a while and play with them.' And the Witch says, 'Surprise! I'm a witch!' Well, it *would've* been a surprise if I hadn't cocked the whole thing up – 'I will grant your wish cos you shared your sandwiches with me. But be warned… being a dolphin is so wonderful that – if you stay one for too long – you might forget that you're a boy. So listen carefully. I'm gonna to tell you a magic word that will change you back. Only *you* can change yourself back. No one else can do it for you. To be safe, make sure you say this magic word as soon as you see the sun begin to set. The word is … Karamazoo! You have to say it three times. You understand? You have to say Karamazoo three times before the dolphin form takes you over forever and you forget who you really are. Do you understand?' 'I understand,' said the boy. And so the Witch waves a magic wand or something and flash-bang-wallop – the Boy turns into a dolphin and he's off splashing and squeaking. What a wonderful time he has. He's having such a blinding time that when he sees the sky turning red with sunset he thinks, Sod that! I'll give it a few more minutes. And a few minutes later he thinks, Sod that! A few more minutes. And so it goes on. Until the sky is full of stars. But by then it's too late. Because now the Boy has forgotten he has ever been a boy. And when he hears the sound of a woman calling for her son … in the forest … he didn't even realise … it was … his Mum …

Slight pause.

It's not the waterworks or anything. It's just the hay fever. I always get it. Bloody nuisance.

Looks at phone.

It's just plain rude, I reckon. Holly not phoning back. She must have got my messages. She checks her messages every two minutes. I've *seen* her. Her brother's not well, you see. He's in a wheelchair. He's got that ... muscular thing wrong with him. You know? When you twist and turn and can't talk properly. Like you're being electrocuted. Holly's always worrying about him.

Slight pause.

I've brought a photo to show her. Me. A few years ago.

Slight pause.

I'm gonna shock you now. Fasten your safety belts – Once ... I was *not* an alpha. I was a ... well, an Invisible, I guess. I used to go to school – my *old* school – and I'd sit at the back of the class and no one used to talk to me except Josh and we – ... Okay! Another shock! Those with heart problems should take their medication now. I used to be friends with Josh the Geek. His mum was best mates with my mum so ... What can I say? It was another life! Things change. We have to move on. I've tried to help Josh. I've offered advice. It's not my fault he hasn't got what it takes! I can't be responsible for the likes of him, for chrissakes. I've got enough problems of my own.

Slight pause.

I could give Brooke a call! She's my sort of female equivalent at school. The alpha female. I could give Brooke a call and she'd be here – whooosh!

Slight pause.

You know what really hacked me off. They knocked the launderette down. Where Mum used to work. Just three weeks after she died. Three weeks! They demolished the whole street. Everything's just rubble now.

Slight pause.

I went onto it once. The demolition site. They'd put a fence all round it but … there was a gap.

Slight pause.

I remember … Cold … It's snowing … I have to be careful where I walk … Look! That bit of wall … It's from the launderette … I recognise the paint … Mum liked the colour … She said it was cheerful … And I stand there. In the snow and rubble. Just looking at this bit of wall. I can feel the tears freezing on my face. And I think, I'm gonna change! … I'm gonna be different from now on … I'm not gonna be Invisible anymore. I wanna be like those guys down at the cafe. I wanna wear the clothes they wear. I wanna walk like them. Talk like them. I'm gonna change! I know what to do! Soon as New Year hit's I'm down the gym. Every night. I want muscles. I'll do crunches! Bicep curls! Chest press! New body! New hair! Crunches! Bicep curls! Chest press! New name! New walk! Crunches! Bicep! Chest! Bury the old me! Bury him deep! Who wants to be a person who stands in rubble with frozen tears on their face? Not me! No way! I'm Ace now. Alpha male. I don't need any of you. I don't need *anyone*.

Pause.

That's it! Her time's up!

Dials on phone.

I'm not hanging round! I'm phoning Danny. She's had her chance! She can rot in hell for all I care – (*into phone*) Danny-boy, what's the story? … Course I'm alright. You know me. Where are you? Well, wait there I'm coming over. What you say I give Brooke a call and get her to bring Anika and the four of us can have some fun together, eh? … Yeah? You up for it, mate? … You got it! See you in ten minutes!

Hangs up and dials another number.

This is more like it! I want some action! I don't hang around. Not for no one – Hey! Brooke-baby! … Well, I haven't seen those sexy eyes of yours since history and I'm feeling a bit lonely … Mmm, that's good … Danny was wondering if you and Anika

wanna join us for a – Okay! We'll meet you at the cafe. Twenty
minutes!

Hangs up.

What did I tell you? Whooosh! Oh, yesss! I can feel some serious
dancing coming on.

Starts dancing.

You like that? Eh? I could be on telly I reckon. I tell you, when I
hit the floor at *Kinky Gerlinky's* – that's the local haunt. Don't ask
me. I didn't name it – when I'm on that floor … it clears!

Phone rings.

Well, would you believe it, eh? Holly. The Princess of Too Late!
– What d'you want? … No! No bloody excuses! I don't bloody
care if your brother had a fall or if … if he was struck by bloody
lightening. This whole thing's a big set up anyway. Didn't you
realise that? Nah? Well, let me clarify the situation for you.
There's a pig party going on tonight. Know what that is? The
winner is the guy who can bring along the ugliest girl! And I tell
you, if I'd walked in with you on me arm I'd've won hands down.

Slight pause.

She hung up! Bloody nerve! Turned the waterworks on she did. I
don't give a toss. I'm an alpha … the girl's toilets … third cubicle
… I told you, covered … And when I dance … floor clears … I've
got a reputation! Who does she think I am, eh? … Who does she
… who does she … think I am …?

Slight pause.

Karamazoo … Karamazoo … Karamazooo …

Blackout.

Fairytaleheart

Listen,
and you will realize
we are not made from cells or atoms.
We are made from stories.

Mia Couto

Fairytaleheart was first performed at Hampstead Theatre, London, on 27 January 1998 with the following cast and creative team:

Gideon   Zoot Lynam
Kirsty   Victoria Shalet

Director   Philip Ridley
Designer   Jessica Stack
Lighting   Tim Mitchell
Sound   John A. Leonard
Dialect Coach   Barbara Houseman

Characters

Kirsty
Gideon

An abandoned community centre in the East End of London. Most of the windows are broken and boarded over (concealing the snowy, winter evening outside) so what is about to be described is, for the moment, barely visible.

A couple of old chairs, several boxes, a table and a lot of scattered detritus. The table is covered with painting materials: brushes, tubes of paint, spray paint, whatever is needed to have created –

The fairytale backdrop etc. This has been made by adapting and painting found objects: a pile of boxes have become a mountain; an old mantelpiece, a cave; a sheet of corrugated iron, a river; a large mirrorball, a sun or moon. Also depicted are birds, flowers and butterflies. There is also a mirror on the floor, giving the impression of a pond.

The general effect is of a magical landscape, somewhere between a painting and sculpture. This magical quality will eventually intensify with the shimmering light of –

Candles. These are everywhere on stage: across the floor, on tables. Candles of all shapes and sizes. Most are in coloured-glass containers (painted jars etc). They are all, of course, unlit at present.

The entrance to the community hall unlocks and –

Kirsty *enters. She is fifteen years old and carrying a bag in one hand and a torch in the other. She is shivering against the cold outside. Hardly surprising considering her 'party-best' clothing: dress decorated with silver sequins, silver stilettos and a short, white, fake-fur coat. Her hair is neatly styled and highlighted with glitter-gel. She's tried hard to make an impression and she's succeeded.*

Kirsty *closes the door behind her and switches the torch on.*

She treads carefully round the candles, then shines the torch over backdrop.

The light refracts off the mirrorball.

Slight pause.

Kirsty *puts bag down.*

She picks up a brush ... dips it into some paint.

She's adding colour to one of the butterflies as –

The entrance noisily unlocks and –

Gideon *enters. He is fifteen years old and carrying a well-worn bag in one hand and a torch (currently unlit) in the other. His hair is longish and aspires to be dreadlocks. He is well insulated against the cold: a thick and baggy (albeit frayed) jumper, a couple of coats, scarf, gloves and paint-splattered boots. Nothing really goes together but – on him – it works.*

Kirsty *hurriedly turns her torch off and puts brush down.*

Gideon   Who ... who's there?

Closes door and fumbles to light torch.

Who are you?

Slight pause.

I do not mean you any harm.

Kirsty   You don't mean me any –

Turns on her torch.

What *are* you prattling on about?

Gideon *turns on his torch and approaches stage.*

Gideon   ... You're Kirsty.

Kirsty   How d'you know my name?

Gideon   Must have heard it around.

Kirsty   Careful! My eyes!

Flinches at his torchlight.

Gideon   Sorry.

Aims torch away.

You live in the block of flats by the playground, don't you?

Kirsty   If you call a climbing frame surrounded by dog turds a playground, then, yes, that's where I live. Heard that around too, did you?

Gideon   Must have.

Kirsty   You'll be telling me my flat number next.

Gideon   Thirteen.

Kirsty   You been spying on me?

Gideon   No.

Starts removing coats, gloves and scarf.

Unlucky for some, eh?

Kirsty   … What?

Gideon   Thirteen.

Kirsty   I'm not superstitious.

Slight pause.

Gideon   How did you get in?

Kirsty   I unlocked the door.

Gideon   With what?

Kirsty   What d'you think? A key!

Gideon   The only key belongs to me.

Kirsty   Correction. It belongs to your Dad.

Gideon   He's the new caretaker of the estate.

Kirsty   I know.

Gideon   *You* been spying on *me*?

Kirsty   It's a small estate.

Slight pause.

Gideon   So where did you get *your* key from?

Kirsty   You get a degree in being nosy or something? Spanish Inquisition'd give me an easier bloody time.

Gideon   Don't tell me if you don't want to.

Slight pause.

Kirsty   It's my Mum's, if you must know.

Gideon   Your Mum died, didn't she?

Kirsty   You *asking* me or *telling* me?

Slight pause.

Yes, she died. Two years ago. Two years and seven months.

Slight pause.

Before she got sick she used to help out here. Help out – what am I saying? She *ran* the place.

Gideon   When it was a community centre?

Kirsty   That's right. It used to be so … wonderful here. People came to have tea and gossip. Or play bingo. Disco for kids. Mum knew everyone's name. This was her … her …

Gideon   Her kingdom.

Kirsty   … It was.

Gideon   I've heard people on the estate talk about your mum. She was real popular, they say. Beautiful too.

Slight pause.

Kirsty   Bloody hell, it's like a fridge in here.

Gideon   There's no electric.

Kirsty   I know.

Gideon   Then you should have dressed properly.

Kirsty   I *am* dressed properly. I'm just not dressed … *suitably*.

Gideon   You're welcome to one of my coats.

Kirsty   … They look a bit damp.

Gideon   My jumper, then. It's warm with body heat.

Kirsty   … I'd rather not.

Gideon   But your lips are turning blue.

Kirsty   Must be the lipstick.

Gideon   Your legs must be freezing.

Kirsty   You leave my legs out of this.

Gideon   You need thermal tights.

Kirsty   I do *not* need –

Gideon   *I'm* wearing thermal pants.

Kirsty   Thank you for sharing that with me – If you keep shining that thing in my eyes I'll thump you.

Gideon   You're shining yours.

Slight pause.

Slowly, they both avert their torches.

Gideon   It's snowing outside.

Kirsty   So that's what that white stuff's called.

Gideon   You have to be careful about hypothermia when it's like this.

Kirsty   Really?

Gideon   You want something warm to drink?

Takes flask from his bag.

Kirsty   No, thank you.

Gideon   It's peppermint tea with a drop of lavender oil.

Kirsty   And that's supposed to tempt me, is it?

Gideon   Lavender helps you relax.

Kirsty   I *am* bloody relaxed!

Gideon *pours himself a drink from flask.*

He takes a few noisy slurps.

Kirsty *glances at him, irritated.*

Gideon *takes a sandwich from his bag.*

Gideon   Something to eat?

Kirsty   I dread to ask. What is it?

Gideon   Tofu and pine nut sandwich.

Kirsty   Haven't you got anything as basic as crisps and a Coke?

Gideon   Not on me, no.

Kirsty   I'm not hungry.

Gideon *takes a bite from the sandwich.*

He eats as noisily as he drinks.

Kirsty'*s irritation increases. Until –*

Kirsty   Must you?

Gideon   What?

Kirsty   Eat … like that!

Gideon   Like what?

Slight pause.

I'll save the rest for later.

Puts sandwich and flask back in bag.

The cold does amazing things! Don't you think? On the way here the snot up my nose froze. It was funny – I sneezed and this rock hard bogey shot out. Lethal it was. Like a bullet – Voosh!

Kirsty   Killed by a frozen bogey. The cherry on the cake of my day.

Slight pause.

Gideon   Snow makes everything look beautiful.

Kirsty   Take more than snow to make this dump of an estate beautiful.

Gideon   You're wrong … Snow falling in the night sky. Like … ooo, let's think. Like twinkling bits of starlight. How's that? And as it falls it changes colour. The street lights – They turn the snow orange and yellow. Like burning feathers. Yes! It settles. The grey concrete – it's gone. The cracked pavement – gone. Supermarket trolleys – gone. Piles of rubbish – gone. In their place? A twinkling wonderland. When you walk – crunch, crunch, crunch.

Slight pause.

Your eyes look a bit bloodshot.

Kirsty   … It's the cold. Makes them water.

Gideon   Looks like you've been crying to me.

Kirsty   Well, I haven't.

Gideon   Well, it looks like it.

Kirsty   Well, appearances can be deceptive.

Gideon   Yes. They can … Wanna handkerchief?

Takes handkerchief from his pocket.

Kirsty   Ugh! No! I've got a clean one thank you.

Rummages in her bag.

Gideon   You going to the launderette?

Kirsty   Eh? What?

Gideon   All those clothes in your bag.

Kirsty   Oh … no.

Gideon   … Hope that's not *real* fur.

Indicating her coat.

Kirsty   This? Oh … it's baby seal. I culled it myself – Of course it's not real fur! What d'you think I am?

Slight pause.

Gideon   I'll light the candles. It'll make everything feel warmer. Mind over matter and all that.

Starts to light candles.

Kirsty   I've never *seen* so many.

Gideon   Every time I come I bring a few more. Some are amazing. Look at this one. Got gold bits in it.

Kirsty   What's that smell?

Gideon   It's aromatic.

Kirsty   Harry – what?

Gideon   They smell of roses.

Holds candle out for **Kirsty** *to smell.*

Slight pause.

Kirsty *smells candle.*

Gideon   You've got bits in your hair.

Kirsty   … What?

Gideon   Sparkling bits.

Kirsty   Oh, that's the hair gel. It's special. Got glitter in it. What did you think it was? Metallic dandruff?

Gideon   No, I didn't think that.

Slight pause.

Kirsty   Well, I dread to think what's in your hair. When was the last time you washed it?

Gideon   Hair don't need washing. It cleans itself. The body's natural oils keep it healthy. Have a feel.

Kirsty   You keep your natural oils to yourself.

Gideon   Don't you like the style?

Kirsty   Oh, it's a *style,* is it?

Gideon   Dreadlocks – well, almost. Sort of.

Kirsty   Dirty rat's tails – well, totally. Definitely.

Gideon   … My name's Gideon.

Kirsty   I know.

Gideon   You *have* been spying on me.

Kirsty   Oh, don't start all that again. As I said, small estate. New face. 'Who's that?' 'Oh, that's the new caretaker's son. His name is …' blah, blah, blah.

Gideon   The caretaker is *not* my Dad.

Kirsty   What?

Gideon   My *real* Dad left me and Mum years ago. I was a baby. Never seen him since. Or heard from him. Can't remember what he looks like or anything. Mum had a photograph once but she burnt it. Don't blame her. I'd have done the same if someone said, 'I love you', one day, then packed their bags and cleared off the next, without so much as a 'Take care of yourself'. So … well, it was just me and Mum after that. Until she met this man. A few months ago. Love at first sight or some such gobbledygook. Mum just looked at him and … Pow! She sort of … changed. You know? Before she met this man … we agreed on everything, me and Mum. We'd have a laugh about things together and stuff. Now she only laughs with this man and … oh, I don't mind! Not a bit. Anyway! Where was I … ? Yes! That's it! This man was just about to start a new job. Caretaker. Here. So … well, blah, blah, blah as you'd say.

Kirsty *takes unlit candle from table and approaches* **Gideon**.

Kirsty   Let me help.

Gideon   Sorry?

Kirsty   The candles.

Gideon *lights* **Kirsty***'s candle.*

She starts lighting other candles.

Kirsty   Where were you living before? When it was just you and your Mum?

Gideon   Oh, lots of places. Couple of squats. Didn't like those much. Toilets didn't work. We had to do everything in a bucket then throw the gunk down the drain in the street. Sometimes the big bits wouldn't go down and we had to –

Kirsty   I think I can guess the rest.

Slight pause.

Gideon   We lived next to an empty warehouse once. Every Saturday night people would have a rave. Ever been to one?

Kirsty   A rave? No.

Gideon   Music's so loud. Deafening. Used to make my bed shake. Real poltergeist stuff. Amazing.

Kirsty   Didn't you complain?

Gideon   Why? Only people dancing.

Kirsty   Must have kept you awake, though.

Gideon   Sleep through anything, me. You like dancing?

Takes small music player from bag.

Got some amazing music here!

Kirsty   I'm not into music.

Gideon   How can you not be into music? It's like saying, 'I'm not into picking my nose.'

Kirsty   Well, I'm not into picking my nose either.

Gideon   No, but you *do* it. Being into it or not's got nothing to do with it. You just do it. Same with music.

Kirsty   Music and snot. Why have I never seen the connection before?

Gideon   Wanna know the noisiest place me and Mum ever lived?

Kirsty   Not really.

Gideon   Under a flyover. Traffic all night. I slept through a car crash once. Police sirens, ambulance, everything.

Kirsty   How come?

Gideon   Told you – sleep through anything, me.

Kirsty   I meant, how come you were living under a flyover?

Gideon   Oh. We were in a caravan. Staying with some friends of Mum's.

Kirsty   Gypsies?

Gideon   Not really. Just … well, just people with a 'no fixed abode' lifestyle. They gave me and Mum a caravan to ourselves. They let me paint it. I put stars and comets and rainbows all over. Looked amazing. At night we'd sit round a little campfire. Mum'd tell stories. She tells the most amazing things my Mum. I loved that place. It was right beside a canal too. I love the sound of running water, don't you?

Kirsty   I've … I've never really thought about it.

Gideon   I remember one night. Lying in Mum's arms. By the campfire. Everything a flickering orange. And … oh, as I lay there, the sound of the traffic seemed to change. Wasn't traffic any more. It was tropical insects. Jungle sounds. And I imagined the concrete pillars of the flyover were gigantic tree trunks. And the canal was a vast river. Like the Nile or something. Full of crocodiles and hippos. And I imagined all the exotic birds asleep in the undergrowth. Flamingoes, cockatoos, parrots. And the insects. Beautiful, glittering things. Butterflies with wings all colours of the rainbow. And then … then I actually felt something gently touch my fingertips. Guess what it was?

Kirsty   … A butterfly?

Gideon   A rat!

Kirsty   No!

Gideon   The biggest rat you've ever seen. Pink tail. Yellow teeth. It'd crawled out of the canal and was nibbling at my thumbnail.

Kirsty   Hope you killed it.

Gideon   Why? Wasn't hurting anyone.

Kirsty   Bet your Mum was glad to get out of that caravan and come here.

Gideon   She was in love. She'd have gone anywhere and been happy.

Kirsty   But … how did *you* feel?

Gideon   Oh, I can live anywhere, me. Squat, warehouse, council flat –

Kirsty   No, no! Your Mum being with this new bloke. Didn't it bother you?

Gideon   … I'm glad Mum's happy.

Kirsty   That's not what I asked.

Slight pause.

Gideon   Turn your torch off!

Kirsty   What? Oh, yes.

They both turn their torches off.

All the candles are lit now.

Gideon   Magic or what?

Kirsty *and* **Gideon** *look at the candlelit space.*

Kirsty   It *does* feel a bit warmer.

Gideon   Sweltering, me.

Removes jumper to reveal his T-shirt.

Kirsty *gazes at him.*

Gideon   Wh-what's wrong?

Kirsty   Oh … there's a … a hole in your shirt.

Gideon   There's lots of holes. See? One in my jeans too.

Bends over to reveal hole near his backside.

Good for ventilation. When I fart it –

Kirsty   That's quite enough, thank you.

Gideon *takes some painting materials to the mirror on floor.*

He starts mixing paint.

Kirsty   You haven't spoken to many girls, have you?

Gideon   What?

Kirsty   Girls!

Gideon   Girls!? Oh … sure! Zillions of times!

Slight pause.

Kirsty   What you doing?

Gideon   Mixing paint.

Kirsty   No! Here! All this!

Slight pause.

Gideon   A few weeks ago, when I first got here, I thought the whole estate was … well, amazing. Honestly. And this man Mum had met –

Kirsty   Her caretaker boyfriend.

Gideon   This man had the keys to … oh, everywhere! One key … one key let me into vast underground chambers. Where boilers vibrated and buzzed. Like … sleeping giants! Another key took me to the highest roof I'd ever been on. The view goes on for miles. At night the city lights up like a ... a billion flickering candles. All different colours. Another key –

Kirsty   Let you in here.

Gideon   It felt so ... so safe and comfortable. You know? Warm with all the people who'd used this place. To drink tea and gossip. Bingo. Disco.

Kirsty   ... You *felt* that?

Gideon   So I asked this man if I could keep the key and –

Kirsty   You started to come here.

Gideon   Every evening.

Kirsty   Eight o'clock.

Gideon   On the dot. Not that you've been spying on me, of course.

Kirsty   And you're making this – what?

Indicates backdrop etc.

Slight pause.

Gideon   Just think ... imagine! This place – all the rubbish taken out. Windows mended. Walls given a lick of paint. Something bright and cheerful. Floor, swept and polished. Perhaps a carpet. Above, lights – oh, yeah, the electrics back on. And up here, on the stage ... we're doing a play or something. And out there ...

Indicates audience.

The audience! I can imagine them. Their faces. See them almost. Can you?

Kirsty   ... No.

Gideon   You're not trying hard enough.

Kirsty *looks out into audience with* **Gideon**.

Gideon   They're out there!

Pause.

Hear them?

Kirsty   ... No.

Gideon   Concentrate.

Kirsty   I am. And I can't.

Gideon   I'm sure if you try –

Kirsty   Don't push it!

Slight pause.

Gideon   Well ... one day they'll be out there for real. The
audience. And this place – it will be a theatre. That's it. Amazing,
eh?

Kirsty   You *are* bonkers.

Gideon   I believe if you ... if you *show* people something
interesting then they'll *take* an interest.

Kirsty   Who said that? Your Mum?

Gideon   What if she did?

Kirsty   Listen. If you *show* people round here something
interesting, they'll *steal* it. That's if it *was* interesting in the first
place. Which all this, believe me, is not.

Gideon   But ... but people ... people –

Kirsty   You don't know the first thing about people. You know
what people want? What they *really* want? TV. Betting shop. Flash
car. Getting drunk.

Gideon   But ... but I want to give them something else too.

Kirsty   What? A bunch of poncey actors?

Gideon   No, no. We can do our *own* stuff. Write it, act it. Me,
you, my Mum, your Dad –

Kirsty   My *Dad!* Ha!

Gideon   Please don't 'Ha!'. *Please.*

Slight pause.

Let me … try to explain.

Kirsty   … It's all yours.

Slight pause.

Well?

Gideon   I'm trying to remember … Got it! Imagine this: you're a member of a tribe in the middle of a jungle –

Kirsty   I'm *what?*

Gideon   Give me a chance … You're a member of a tribe in the middle of a jungle. The date – it has no meaning for you. Why? Because things have remained the same for millenniums. Since the beginning of time. And for you – for you in particular – all your life has been the same. You live with … with your Dad. In that mud hut over there. See it? Since your Mum died you look after your Dad. You fetch water from the nearby spring. You fish in the river. Your Dad's everything. See the hut yet?

Kirsty   … Yes.

Gideon   And then … a scream! Out in the jungle.

Kirsty   What is it?

Gideon   Someone's been killed.

Kirsty   Who?

Gideon   A member of the tribe.

Kirsty   How?

Gideon   There's a monster in the jungle. Some hideous thing. Claws. Teeth.

Kirsty   Perhaps a giant rat, eh?

Gideon   Very likely. And this giant rat is knocking off members of your tribe one by one. At night you tremble in fear as the giant rat howls and roars. What d'you think we should do?

Kirsty   We've got to kill it.

Gideon   So you and the rest of your tribe get together. You arm yourself with sharpened lengths of bamboo.

Kirsty   Is that *all*?

Gideon   'Fraid so. You scared?

Kirsty   A little.

Gideon   But you've got to go.

Kirsty   Don't know if I can.

Gideon   Aha! So that night the Witchdoctor sits the tribe round a fire. The Witchdoctor gives everyone a … a relaxing drink made from the pussy boils of giant frogs.

Hands her an imaginary drink.

Have a sip.

Kirsty   The pussy boils of giant frogs?

Gideon   And a few worms.

Slowly, **Kirsty** *drinks.*

Gideon   And – as the pus 'n' worm mixture takes a dreamy effect – the Witchdoctor says, 'As you all know, our tribe is being threatened by the terrible giant rat. It must be killed. I know you are afraid. But you must face this fear. So – listen … imagine you have gone into the jungle. Hear the jungle sounds. Smell the smells. Look! There's the giant rat. See its huge teeth and gigantic claws. Oh, no! It's seen you. It's charging straight at you. You want to run. But you don't. You raise your bamboo spear. The giant rat's getting closer. Aim. Closer! Throw! The spear punctures the creature's heart. It screams. Birds erupt from trees. Then … silence. The giant rat is dead.'

Slight pause.

The next morning the tribe goes into the jungle. In the distance they can hear the giant rat stomping through the undergrowth. They say, 'In our dreams we have already faced this monster. We are not afraid.'

Slight pause.

Kirsty   … And?

Gideon   There is no 'and'.

Kirsty   You mean … that's it?

Gideon   Yes.

Kirsty   And you think that explains something?

Gideon   … *Doesn't* it?

Kirsty   Er … not to me.

Gideon   But it's *supposed* t … to help make clear –

Kirsty   Listen, I don't know what orbit you're in, but tell me when the shuttle lands and we might actually have a conversation.

Gideon   *You* listen! You live on an estate. An estate full of cracked concrete. Graffiti. Ruined community centres. You know the date very well. It's one of the millions of facts that fill your mind. You get these facts from computers. Television. Newspapers. Internet. You do not believe in giant rats. And yet – you're afraid. You don't know why. But something scares you. Oh, it doesn't have sharp teeth or claws or a gigantic, pink tail. But still you're so, so afraid. The fear makes you feel so alone. Makes you cry. Makes you want to run away.

Pause.

Gideon *starts mixing paints again.*

Kirsty *watches him for a while.*

Then, slowly, she goes to him.

Kirsty   I like that colour.

Gideon   Hmm.

Slight pause.

Kirsty   It's very bright.

Gideon   Hmm.

Slight pause.

Kirsty   Like sunshine.

Gideon   … It's called cadmium yellow.

Kirsty   What's that one?

Gideon   Crimson lake. Amazing names, eh? Like magic spells.
Rose madder. Monestial blue. Raw sienna.

Kirsty   Eye of newt.

Gideon   Toe of frog.

Goes to start painting, then –

The butterfly!

Kirsty   What?

Gideon   A couple of days ago. Did you come in here? When I
wasn't here?

Kirsty   … Wh-what if I did?

Gideon   That butterfly.

Points.

Kirsty   … The blue and yellow one.

Gideon   You painted it, didn't you.

Kirsty   What if I did?

Gideon   Oh, no.

Kirsty   I only came here to see what you were up to but … well,
I saw all the paints and brushes. I couldn't resist. Have I spoilt it?

Gideon   No, no, it's not that. I was hoping a ghost did it.

Kirsty   *'Hoping'* it was a ghost!? Don't you mean *'scared'*?

Gideon   What's to be scared of? A ghost is just a lost spirit. Someone who don't believe they're dead. I was gonna help it. Bring a Ouija board or something. Tell it, 'Sorry, dear spirit, but it's time to travel to the next world.' It's what I thought you were. When I first came in and heard you. A ghost!

Kirsty   That's why you called, 'I mean you no harm,' like that.

Gideon   Got all excited, me.

Kirsty   Sorry to disappoint you.

Gideon   Oh, you're more interesting than a ghost.

Slight pause.

Why don't you help me?

Kirsty   I'd … I'd ruin it.

Gideon   Your yellow and blue butterfly is very … promising.

Kirsty   More interesting than a ghost and a promising butterfly. Certainly is my night for flattery.

Gideon *holds out brush and paint.*

Slight pause.

Kirsty *removes her coat and lays it on top of her bag.*

She takes brush and paint and goes to backdrop.

She hesitates …

Kirsty   What shall I do?

Gideon   Paint some flowers over there.

Kirsty   Where? Just here?

Gideon   No. That's the cave.

Kirsty   Oh, I *see*. The *cave*.

Gideon   Do it there! That's it!

Slight pause.

He doesn't like flowers, you see.

Kirsty   Who?

Gideon   The Wizard?

Kirsty   *What* Wizard?

Gideon   That one there!

Kirsty   … I don't see him.

Gideon   He's in the Magic Cave.

Kirsty   Silly me.

Slight pause.

Kirsty *goes to paint, then hesitates again…*

Gideon   Here! Practice on this first.

He puts sheet of paper in front of **Kirsty***.*

Kirsty *still hesitates.*

Gideon   Just relax. Imagine soaking in a hot bath. Then think, flowers! Then let the thought travel out of your head and down your arm. Like an electric current. Buzz. Then out! Splat! Paint it!

Kirsty   … Relax. Think. Buzz. Splat. Paint.

Gideon   All there is to it.

Kirsty *closes her eyes.*

Gideon   That's it. Relax … Think, flowers … Let it build up … *Feel* it … *Feel* it …

Kirsty *starts to tremble.*

Gideon   Electric current … buzzing … buzzing …

Kirsty *trembles some more.*

Gideon   Now let it travel down your arm … That's it … Build it up … That's it … Now – Splat!

With an ecstatic cry, **Kirsty** *starts painting.*

Gideon   See? Easy?

Kirsty   How will I know if I'm doing it right?

Gideon   Oh, you'll know. It's like kissing. Sometimes you're smooching away and you're thinking, My nose is in the way! My teeth are too big! Where do I put my hands? That's a wrong kiss. But when it's going right … Oh, I bet everything falls into place. No worries. Just an amazing – You *have* been kissed, haven't you?

Kirsty   … Kissed?! Me!? Zillions of times!

Slight pause.

Kirsty *continues painting.*

Gideon *resumes his own painting.*

Kirsty   Wh … what's the play going to be about?

Gideon   No idea yet.

Kirsty   You must have.

Gideon   Why? … Oh! The backdrop and stuff! Well, that's just the basics. When Mum makes up her stories they always have a King, Queen, Prince, Princess, Castle, Forest –

Kirsty   Wizard?

Gideon   Exactly!

Kirsty   Fairytales?

Gideon   Oh, more than that. The stories are a way of helping me … you know, with all the moving and new faces and stuff. Mum says they're a way of expressing what's really in your heart. Your fairytaleheart, she calls it.

Kirsty   Fairytaleheart?

Gideon   Amazing, eh? You see, if Mum told me a story about

... well, a Prince who was misunderstood by everyone except the Queen. Then I'd know that the Queen was my Mum and ... well – You've got some paint on your skirt.

Kirsty   Oh, no! It's brand new.

Gideon   I've got something to get it off.

Gets some rags, etc.

Sit down.

Kirsty *sits on chair.*

Gideon *kneels in front of her.*

He starts dabbing paint from her skirt.

Slight pause.

Gideon   Looks like you.

Kirsty   ... What?

Gideon   The flower.

Kirsty   How can a flower look like someone?

Gideon   It's got your ... your spirit.

Slight pause.

Kirsty   It's my birthday today.

Gideon   Aries! That explains it!

Kirsty   I don't believe in horoscopes.

Slight pause.

What're Aries like anyway?

Gideon   Fiery. Dominating. Argumentative.

Kirsty   I'm not bloody argumentative.

Gideon   Happy birthday.

Slight pause.

Kirsty Dad organized a birthday party for me. Back at our flat. It's why I'm in this outfit. Had my hair done special too.

Slight pause.

Do you like it?

Gideon Not sure about the metallic dandruff.

Kirsty Lie! Okay? It's called being nice to someone. I fish for a compliment. You give one. Got it?

Gideon … Try again.

Kirsty Do you like my hair?

Gideon It's amazing!

Kirsty Thank you.

Slight pause.

I ran out of the party. It was horrible.

Gideon Life's too short for horrible parties.

Indicates clean dress.

There! Good as new.

He resumes painting.

Slight pause.

Kirsty Ever since Mum died … it's just been me and Dad. We did everything together. Not that we did much … Oh, I don't want to talk about it.

Gideon *has stopped painting to listen.*

Now he resumes painting, absently humming.

Slight pause.

Kirsty Some people must have thought it boring. Going to the pictures with your Dad. Not me. I loved it … Oh, I don't want to talk about it.

Gideon *has stopped painting to listen.*

Now he resumes painting and humming.

Slight pause.

Kirsty   Then one day, we go into the supermarket. Dad's pushing the trolley. I'm putting things in. Same as usual. And, suddenly, I turn round – the trolley's gone! 'Dad!' Up and down the aisles. 'Dad!' There he is! At the checkout. Talking to … A woman! Look at her! Hair styled by a lawnmower. Colour out of a bottle. Eyelashes fluttering so much it's a wonder they don't issue a gale warning. And her tits! Talk about padded bra. You could land a helicopter on them. And Dad! Look at him! Lapping it up … Oh, I don't want to talk about it! Hear me? I don't want to talk about it!

Gideon *has stopped painting to listen.*

Now he resumes painting and humming.

Kirsty   Aren't you interested?

Gideon   You don't want to talk about it.

Kirsty   Don't be so obliging! *Ask* me something.

Slight pause.

Gideon   Do you think I should grow a goatee?

Kirsty   … What?

Gideon   A little beard. Just on my chin. I'm sure I've got enough whiskers. Feel?

Kirsty   I'm not bothered about that!

Gideon   But you said ask you something.

Kirsty   Not about bloody whiskers! About … her! That woman. Dad's floozie. Say something about her!

Gideon   … I think she's nice.

Kirsty   You … you don't know her.

Gideon   I know who you mean. Seen her in the supermarket. She wears a ribbon in her hair.

Kirsty   Mutton dressed as lamb!

Gideon   Good figure.

Kirsty   Deformed!

Gideon   Always smiling.

Kirsty   Demented!

Gideon   Jolly!

Kirsty   Oh, yes, she's jolly all right. Got Dad wrapped round her little bloody finger. Like a couple of school kids, they are. You should have seen them. At my party too! Canoodling. Nibbling each other's ears! Disgusting! And every time she looks at my Dad she clutches her chest and goes, 'Ooo! You make my heart go boom-diddy, boom-diddy.'

Gideon   'Boom-diddy, boom-diddy'?

Kirsty   'Boom-diddy, boom-diddy'! Yuk! I tell you, if her brains were dynamite, they wouldn't blow frozen bogeys out of her nose.

Gideon   Well, I don't agree. I'm sorry. And you know what else I think? You're being a tad unreasonable. I've seen your Dad with her. They look good for each other. So my advice: relax. Chill out. Go with the flow.

Continues painting.

Pause.

Suddenly, **Kirsty** *puts on her coat and picks up her bag and torch.*

Gideon   What you doing?

Kirsty   Going.

Gideon   Where?

Kirsty   Anywhere.

Gideon   But … you can't just run away.

Kirsty   Watch me! You weren't at the party. You didn't see them. My Dad and that woman. Bloody embarrassing. I couldn't bear it! I packed a few things and got out! Bet they haven't even missed me. I should have run miles away fast as possible. Not come here.

Gideon   Why *did* you come here?

Kirsty   Not to see *you*, if that's what you're thinking. I wouldn't want to see you for all the crackers in Karamazoo.

Gideon   All the crackers in what?

Kirsty   It's what my Dad says. I love you more than all the crackers in Karamazoo! You're Daddy's little Princess! Daddy wouldn't swap you for all the crackers in – Oh, why am I telling you this! You don't bloody care.

Strides towards exit.

Gideon   You … you got any money?

Kirsty   No.

Gideon   Then how you going to –

Kirsty   I don't know! All I know is … I can't stay here … I'm not needed … Who'll care? I'll sleep in shop doorways … Others do it … I don't mind the cold … I don't … Oh, I don't know …

Has gradually come to a halt and hovers by exit.

Gideon   Before … before you go – because I can see you're determined to go, and I wouldn't stop that – but, before you go, will you help me with something.

Slight pause.

Please.

Kirsty   … What?

Gideon   A … a story! Yes! That's it! Perhaps we could … oh, I don't know. Make something up. Like Mum makes up her stories. You know? Kings, Queens, Princes, Princesses. We could do it – the two of us. I know you won't be around to see it when the

theatre's finished and everything. You'll be miles away by then.
But … well, when people ask, 'Why did Kirsty run away?' I can
tell them, See the play and you'll understand.'

Pause.

There was once a kingdom called Karamazoo.

Slight pause.

Kirsty   … What's it like?

Gideon   Karamazoo? Oh, it's an amazing place. See for yourself!
Look! Fields of flowers. Distant mountains. A river. Cave. And …
oh, yes, the most perfect butterflies.

Slight pause.

Slowly, **Kirsty** *approaches stage.*

Kirsty   Don't forget the candles.

Gideon   Candles! Of course! Candles! Everywhere.

Kirsty   Why?

Gideon   Because … the Queen has just died. That's it! The
kingdom's in mourning. The Queen was so popular. Everyone
loved her. And now … every place the Queen once visited has
been turned into a shrine. Nothing but candles, candles, candles.
How does that sound? There are crowds of people outside the
castle. They want some word from the King.

Kirsty   He's too upset to speak –

Gideon   Said the Princess.

Takes torch and bag from her.

He helps her out of her coat.

Gideon   Speak, Princess. Please! Your people need you to speak!

Puts chair in middle of stage.

Get up on the balcony and speak.

Kirsty   The balcony?

Gideon   Let me help you, Princess.

Helps **Kirsty** *up on chair.*

Gideon   The Princess! She's going to speak to us!

(*chanting*) Princ-ess! Princ-ess! Princ-ess!

Kirsty   All right, all right!

Gideon   Princ-ess!

Kirsty   Shut up!

Gideon *silences.*

Kirsty   Thank you, people of Karamazoo … I can't begin to explain how much your support means to me.

Gideon   (*in voice of news reporter*) But tell us, Princess, what did you feel when you first heard the news of Her Majesty's sudden death?

Kirsty   It wasn't sudden. She'd been ill for ages. Everyone in … in Karamazoo knows that. They sent flowers. So many. But still … When she finally died, I couldn't believe it.

Gideon   Where were you when you heard?

Kirsty   I was in bed … My Dad woke me. He was crying. He didn't need to tell me what had happened.

Gideon   Tell us, Princess, what do you miss most about the Queen?

Slight pause.

Kirsty   When she cuddled me she smelt of roses. She bought me earrings. Sad songs made her cry. She always got my jokes. She wore a hat with silk flowers … She never complained. Not all the time she was sick. – Oh, I can't do this.

Gideon   One more question, Princess!

Kirsty   Who *are* you anyway?

Gideon   I'm a journalist from the *The Daily Karamazoo*.

Kirsty   The *what*?!

Gideon   Your Highness. Obviously you don't get it in the castle … The rumour is the Queen's last words to you were, 'Look after the King.' Can you confirm this?

Slight pause.

Kirsty   … How do you know?

Gideon   Can you confirm it?

Kirsty   … Yes, it's true.

Gideon   And so the Princess looked after the King. Every morning she cooked him breakfast. She walked with him in the gardens of the castle. She washed his cloak when it got stained with bird droppings. And, at night, as they sat by candlelight, the Princess told the King stories about …

Slight pause.

About?

Kirsty   … My Mum.

Gideon   How everyone loved her.

Kirsty   That's right.

Gideon   How beautiful.

Kirsty   Oh, yes.

Gideon   How he'll never find anyone as perfect as her.

Kirsty   Well, he won't!

Gets small, framed photo from her bag.

Look at her!

Shows photo to **Gideon**.

Kirsty   Tell me I'm wrong! Could he *ever* find *any*one to match – to come even *close* – to someone like that?

Gideon   You won't let him look!

Kirsty   Why would he *want* to look?

Gideon   You want to keep him all to yourself.

Kirsty   Wh-what? No.

Gideon   Just you and him in your own little world. While outside
– look around you! Karamazoo is going down the toilet. A King
can't lock himself away and ignore his people. They need him.
They're calling for him. Listen! (*chanting*) We want the King! We
want the King! We want the King!

Kirsty   You're so selfish. My Dad's still in mourning.

Gideon   But it's been nearly three years!

Kirsty   So what?

Gideon   (*in voice of news reporter*) Princess! There's a rumour
the King has met someone new. Can you confirm this?

Kirsty   … No.

Gideon   No you can't confirm it or no it's not true?

Kirsty   I … I don't want to talk about –

Gideon   Princess! *The Daily Karamazoo* has drawings of the
meeting.

Kirsty   Fairytale paparazzi!?

Gideon   These drawings clearly show the King laughing –
perhaps even hugging – a woman. Take my advice, Princess. It's
best to make a statement now. Before the situation gets out of
control.

Slight pause.

Kirsty   Once a week I go with Dad to … to the forest at the back
of the castle.

Gideon   Good. Carry on, Princess.

Kirsty   We go there to … collect wild berries and apples.

Gideon   Rumour has it the King holds the basket while you pick the berries and apples. Can you confirm this?

Kirsty   It's true.

Gideon   Go on.

Kirsty   … On a recent trip … 'Oh, look, Dad! A squirrel! A red one! How beautiful … Wh-where are you, Dad?' Dad's gone. This has never happened before. 'Dad! Dad!' No sign. Rush to the river! Not there. Rush to the – Ah! There he is! Wait! He's … he's talking to … A woman!

Gideon   The drawings show a woman with big breasts. Can you confirm this?

Kirsty   You can land a … a dragon on them.

Gideon   Bet the King's happy.

Kirsty   Haven't seen him this happy since before Mum – No! Look!

Gideon   What?

Kirsty   Dad's holding her hand. Squeezing! No! They're almost hugging – they *are* hugging! 'Stop it! Dad! Come back to the castle and – What? You want to go strolling with *her*. But you can't – Dad! Don't! Don't!'

Slight pause.

Gideon   Tell us, Princess, how often has the King seen this woman since?

Kirsty   Her toothbrush is in the bathroom.

Gideon   'STOP PRESS! KING'S GIRLFRIEND IN TOOTHBRUSH IN BATHROOM SCANDAL!'

Kirsty   She is *not* his girlfriend.

Gideon   Not for much longer, no! Because rumour has it that, tonight, at your birthday party, the King intends to announce he's getting married.

Kirsty   I didn't tell you that. How ... how could you know?

Gideon   'PRINCESS DOES NOT DENY KING TO REMARRY.'

Slowly, **Kirsty** *sits.*

Gideon *turns ghetto blaster on.*

Dance music starts to play.

Gideon   What a rave, eh? No one does it like the royals.
Amazing music, eh?

Kirsty   The DJ should be shot.

Turns music off.

Gideon   Hang on! Don't you touch my ... Hey! You're the
Princess or something, right?

Kirsty   That's right.

Gideon   How old are you?

Kirsty   Fifteen.

Gideon   I'm fifteen and a half.

Turns music back on.

Like my dancing?

Kirsty   You look like an apoplectic octopus.

Gideon   Thanks! Wow! I'm getting all hot and sweaty. Why
don't you get all hot and sweaty too?

Kirsty   Because I've got a brain.

Gideon   You know what I think?

Kirsty   Tell me.

Gideon   You suffer from ... bodyphobia. Fear of the body's
natural functions. Farting, sweating, burping, sneezing. I bet you
don't even enjoy picking your nose, do you?

Kirsty *turns music down a little.*

Kirsty   Well, you know what you suffer from. *Bodymania.* You enjoy natural functions too much.

Gideon   What's wrong with that?

Kirsty   It's revolting! I've heard you eat! Made me sick!

Gideon   Then try one of these nibbles and show me how a Princess does it.

Offers imaginary plate.

Kirsty   What is it?

Gideon   Delicious! Eat!

Slight pause.

Go on.

Kirsty *eats.*

Gideon   It's a pickled pigeon's head.

Turns music up and continues dancing.

Look! It's the King! And he's with his new girlfriend. Look at them dance! Go for it, my son! Wow! She can really dance.

Kirsty   She's drunk.

Gideon   You could do with a glass of something. Help you relax – Hang on! Something's happening. Must be important! Everyone's stopped dancing.

He turns music off.

Kirsty *and* **Gideon** *stare ahead, listening.*

Gideon   The King's making an announcement. It's about him and he's new girlfriend. Oh! Do you think royal wedding is on the cards?

Slowly, shock spreads over **Kirsty***'s face.*

Gradually, she rises to her feet.

A scream is bubbling up inside her.

Gideon *is nodding and smiling, listening intently. Then –*

Kirsty   (*screaming*) Noooooo!

Gideon *snatches old newspaper from floor.*

Gideon   Extra! Extra! Read all about it 'PRINCESS UPSET BY KING'S MARRIAGE PLANS: The birthday celebrations of the Princess were thrown into disarray last night when the King, a widower, fifty-something –'

Kirsty   Forty-five!

Gideon   '– announced his intention of remarrying. The future new Queen – an apple-grower, thirty-eight – met the King a few months ago and, since then, their relationship has blossomed. A spokesperson for the Palace said, "I'm sure all of Karamazoo will rejoice in His Majesty's new found joy." Everyone, that is, except the Princess who, upon hearing the news, packed a laundry bag full of lace handkerchiefs and tiaras and stormed out of the castle. Rumour has it the Princess has not been seen since. One can only hope that, in such horrible weather, she's packed some warm clothing.'

Slight pause.

So … where are you going?

Kirsty   I don't know.

Gideon   It's your story.

Kirsty   Then I'm lost.

Gideon   For days the Princess roamed the Kingdom of Karamazoo. She didn't know where she was going. And then, one day, she stumbled on a Cave …

He rushes behind mantelpiece.

Slight pause.

Kirsty   Oh, come out.

Gideon   I can't. I'm the Wizard of the Magic Cave.

Slight pause.

Slowly, **Kirsty** *approaches mantelpiece.*

Kirsty   So ... you do wishes, right?

Gideon   You're mistaking me for a genie. Wizards do spells.

Kirsty   Would you do a spell for me?

Gideon   You want the King to stop loving this apple-seller woman, right?

Kirsty   How did you know?

Gideon   I read *The Daily Karamazoo.*

Kirsty   Can you *do* it? Yes or no?

Gideon   Yes! Listen! You must go in search of the ... the legendary Luminous Butterfly of Karamazoo.

Kirsty   The Legendary Luminous Butterfly of Karamazoo?

Gideon   Sounds good, eh? And, when you find it, you will ...

Kirsty   Yes? Come on.

Gideon   ... You'll get your heart's desire!

Slight pause.

Kirsty *looks round stage.*

She cups her hand over one of the painted butterflies.

Gideon *emerges from behind backdrop.*

Kirsty   Found it!

Gideon   Show me.

Kirsty *opens her hands.*

Gideon   That's no Luminous Butterfly.

Kirsty   Yes it is.

Gideon   It's not.

Kirsty   Is!

Gideon   Not! Look at it! It's just your common or garden butterfly. You think the Wizard would call it legendary if you could turn round and find one just like that.

Kirsty   You get a degree in Luminous Butterflies, or something?

Gideon   No. But I *am* a Prince.

Kirsty   A Prince! Ha!

Gideon   Don't 'Ha' me! I told you!

S*light pause.*

I suppose you're some kind of Princess.

Kirsty   Well … yes, actually.

Gideon   Prove it.

Kirsty   … My Dad's a King!

Gideon   Fair enough. As for me … well, here are my references.

Takes pieces of paper from back pocket.

As you can see … rescued this Princess from a Dragon. She says some very nice things. Here: 'Never seen such a cool hairstyle on a Prince.' Rescued this Princess from a hundred years' sleep: 'I'm sure he'll look even more dashing when he grows his goatee.' Rescued this Princess by kissing her –

Kirsty   Oh, so that's what this is all about. You think I'm a helpless Princess in need of kissing – I mean, rescuing.

Gideon   No.

Kirsty   Liar!

Snatches papers from Gideon and rips them up.

Gideon   Look! You're not the only one with problems.

Kirsty   Don't tell me *you've* got problems.

Gideon   Why *shouldn't* I?

Kirsty   What? Mr Relax, chill out, go with the flow? Problems? Ha!

Gideon   (*suddenly flaring*) Don't bloody 'Ha!' You hear me? You think I'm just a bloody joke or something? I've had enough of it. Everybody bloody going 'Ha!' So … just don't 'Ha!' You understand? Just don't 'Ha!' Just … Oh, forget it.

Pause.

Kirsty   … I'm sorry.

Gideon   Forget it, I said!

Slight pause.

Kirsty   You … you can tell me.

Gideon   What?

Kirsty   Your problems.

Gideon   As if you're bothered.

Kirsty   I am. Tell me. Please.

Slight pause.

Please, Prince. The Princess wants to hear.

Gideon   Well … it's my Mum –

Kirsty   The Queen?

Gideon   That's right. The Queen. She's found this … this …

Kirsty   Future King?

Gideon   Yes. That's it!

Kirsty   A King who keeps going 'Ha!'

Gideon   And the Queen doesn't stop him. Before … the Queen and the Prince, we'd read books and paint and tell stories and talk about … oh, amazing things. She wouldn't let anyone go 'Ha!' at me then. But now …

Kirsty   She's fallen in love with the King of Ha!

Gideon   The King of Ha! That's good.

Slight pause.

I thought, I'll build this …

Indicates backdrop.

She'll see it and she'll remember how me and her … how we …
and then she'll … oh, I don't know.

Slight pause.

Kirsty   Go to the Wizard?

Gideon   … What?

Kirsty   The Wizard in the Magic Cave? Why don't you go to him?

Gideon   I … I already did.

Kirsty   What did he say?

Gideon   … He granted me a wish –

Kirsty   You mean a spell.

Gideon   Silly me.

Kirsty   So what did he say? The Wizard. Tell me.

Gideon   He said … if I found the Luminous Butterfly –

Kirsty   You'd get what your heart desires.

Gideon   That's right.

Kirsty   He said the same to me.

Gideon   What a small kingdom.

Slight pause.

Well, good luck, Princess.

He strides away.

Kirsty   What're you doing now?

Gideon   I'm going to search for the Luminous Butterfly.

Kirsty   But … wait!

Gideon *stops.*

Kirsty   Why don't we … search for the Luminous Butterfly together?

Gideon   You don't look like the kind of person who relishes company.

He walks further away.

Kirsty   But I do!

Gideon   You *do*?

Kirsty   … Yes.

Slight pause.

Do *you*?

Gideon   … Let's start searching!

Kirsty and **Gideon** *walk around stage, looking for butterfly.*

Then –

Gideon   (*pointing*) Look at that view!

Kirsty   … What?

Gideon   The field of flowers. Oh, smell the perfume. Roses. And look there! A waterfall! And there – in the river – multicoloured fish … What can you see, Princess?

Slight pause.

Kirsty   I see … birds!

Gideon   I see them too.

Kirsty   Beautiful long tail feathers. So many colours. Cadmium yellow. Monestial blue. Crimson lake.

Gideon   What beautiful things you see, Princess. Oh! You look cold. Here, wear my cloak to keep you warm.

He gets his discarded jumper.

He goes to drape it round **Kirsty**'s *shoulders.*

Gideon   Do you want it?

Kirsty   Yes.

Gideon *drapes jumper round* **Kirsty**'s *shoulders.*

Slight pause.

Gideon *picks up torch and turns it on.*

He points at spot of light.

Gideon   Look! There! See it?

Kirsty   … See what?

Gideon   The Luminous Butterfly!

He darts spot of light all over the place.

Gideon   Look at it go!

Kirsty   Catch it!

Gideon *runs round stage attempting to catch light.*

Kirsty   Go on! That's it! Nearly! Mind the candles! Careful.

Gideon   It's on me! Look! It tickles.

Kirsty   Catch it! Catch it!

Gideon   Where's it gone now?

Kirsty   Behind you.

Gideon   Where?

Kirsty   Still behind you!

Gideon *continues chasing light.*

Much laughter and activity.

Then **Gideon** *turns light off.*

Gideon   It's gone.

Kirsty   Let *me* try next time.

Gideon   You know, Princess, the Wizard once showed me another way of seeing this landscape. He called the field of flowers a ... a concrete playground. And the mountains, tower blocks. And the beautiful pond, a dirty canal. And the fish in the pond – what were they? Well, rats, I guess! And – even though this landscape might sound ugly – it wasn't.

Slight pause.

Kirsty   And, in this landscape, you – a Prince – you could be a caretaker's son.

Gideon   And you – a Princess – you could be the most amazing girl on the estate.

Slight pause.

Gideon *turns torch back on and points.*

Kirsty   My turn!

Gideon   Go on, then. Catch it!

Kirsty *darts round stage, trying to catch spot of light.*

Gideon *keeps it just out of her grasp.*

They're both laughing and giggling.

Gideon   It's on the table! Look!

Kirsty *creeps up to table.*

Gideon   Careful! Don't scare it! It's going to fly to the mountains soon.

Kirsty *lunges for light.*

Gideon *moves light away.*

Kirsty   Not fair!

Gideon   Told you!

Kirsty   Well, you catch it! You seem to know where it's going!

Gideon *starts dashing all over the place.*

He's holding the torch – a soothing spot of light just out of his reach.

Kirsty *laughs more and more at his antics.*

Gideon *jumps off stage.*

He rushes round auditorium.

Then back on stage, and goes behind backdrop.

Kirsty, *helpless with laughter, gradually gets her breath back.*

Kirsty   You caught it?

Slight pause.

Prince?

Slight pause.

Hello?

Looks behind backdrop.

Where are you? … Prince? … So … is that it? It was all just a game! You've gone and left me.

Getting tearful now.

You didn't mean *any* of it?

Weeps.

Pause.

Suddenly, **Gideon** *bursts in from main entrance.*

Gideon   (*brightly*) No luck!

Approaching stage.

Chased it all the way to the waterfall. Then – Whoosh! Gone!

He jumps up on stage.

Kirsty   How did you bloody get back there?

Gideon   I know my way round Karamazoo …

Slight pause.

Wh … what's wrong?

Kirsty   I thought you'd … you'd … Oh, nothing.

Slight pause.

Gideon   I wouldn't leave you.

Kirsty   … You wouldn't?

They stand very close to each other, face to face, almost touching.

Pause.

Gideon *is holding torch between them.*

He turns it on.

Gideon   We've caught it!

Kirsty   The Luminous Butterfly.

Gideon   So now … the Wizard's spell – it'll start working.

Slight pause.

The King – he'll stop loving that woman.

Slight pause.

He'll be all alone again.

Kirsty   He'll have me.

Gideon   Of course. It'll be just you and him. That's what you wanted. Right?

Kirsty   … And what about your Mum? The Queen! She'll stop loving the King of Ha. It'll be just you and her. That's what *you* wanted. Right?

Gideon   … I asked *you* first.

Slight pause.

Well, Princess? … *Well?*

Kirsty   … Come to the party with me.

Gideon   Wh-what?

Kirsty   The party.

Gideon   But. … that's not … I asked you about the *King*, Princess –

Kirsty   Oh, stop all that.

Gideon   … Stop?

Kirsty   Party. Coming?

Gideon   But … I can't just turn up at your –

Kirsty   Of *course* you can! And you won't 'just be' turning up. You'll be with me.

Gideon   But … My hair! Rat's tails!

Kirsty   No one'll mind.

Gideon   My clothes. Holes in T-shirt.

Kirsty   What you panicking for?

Gideon   People will laugh at me!

Kirsty   Stop it!

Gideon   … It's safer here.

Kirsty   … Listen … It's just a party. That's all. The people who'll be there – you know who they are? People from the estate. The *same* people you're making all this for. So stop *talking* about them and *meet* them. That makes sense, doesn't it? … Well, *doesn't* it?

Gideon   … I suppose so.

Kirsty   Okay. So let's try to have a normal conversation about this. Remember how it works? It's the same as when I was fishing

for a compliment. I say something, then you say something nice
back. Ready? … *Ready?*

Gideon   … Mmm.

Kirsty   Here goes … Oh, I do wish I had someone to go to my
party with.

Slight pause.

Gideon   … I'll don't mind going.

Kirsty   Nearly.

Gideon   … I *want* to go.

Kirsty   Closer.

Gideon   I'd *love* to go with you.

Kirsty   Thank you. I'd love to go with you too. Easy, eh?

Gideon   … Hello, Kirsty.

Kirsty   Hello, Gideon.

Slight pause.

Slowly, they lean forward as if to kiss.

Then hesitate ...

Then lean closer.

Hesitate.

Closer.

Then –

Gideon *turns torch off and –*

Gideon   Help me blow out the candles.

From either end of the stage, **Kirsty** *and* **Gideon** *start blowing
out the candles.*

It has a ceremonial, almost ritualistic feel.

Slowly, they both make their way centre stage.

Kirsty   You hungry?

Gideon   Always starving, me.

Kirsty   There's sherry trifle at the party.

Gideon   Sherry trifle's amazing.

Kirsty   Well, this one's not. Dad's girlfriend – I mean fiancée – made it. Keep your mouth shut, though.

Gideon   Don't want to upset her, do we?

Kirsty   Guess not.

They're getting closer and closer.

Gideon   Will you dance with me?

Kirsty   I'm not very good.

Gideon   It's easy. You just relax –

Kirsty   Think!

Gideon   Buzz!

Kirsty   Splat!

Gideon and **Kirsty**   Dance!

Gideon   Exactly! And you'll know when you're doing it right 'cos it'll be just like –

Kirsty   Picking my nose?

Gideon   Kissing.

They're almost together now.

Just a few more candles.

Blow ... darkness.

Blow ... darkness.

Kirsty   I think a goatee *would* suit you.

Gideon   I've got the whiskers.

Kirsty   Let me feel.

They are face to face.

One candle left.

Gently, **Kirsty** *feels* **Gideon**'s *face.*

Slight pause.

They both pick up remaining candle and hold it between them.

Gideon   (*touching his chest*) Boom-diddy, boom-diddy.

Kirsty   (*touching her chest*) Boom-diddy, boom-diddy.

They blow out candle.

Blackout.

Sparkleshark

Behind every mask there is a face,
and behind that a story.

Marty Rubin

Sparkleshark was commissioned by the Royal National Theatre, London, as part of the National Connections Festival 1997. It received its professional premiere at the Royal National Theatre, London, on 7 June 1999 with the following cast and creative team:

Jake	Nitzan Sharron
Polly	Jody Watson
Natasha	Maggie Lloyd-Williams
Carol	Kellie Bright
Russell	Chiwetel Ejiofor
Buzz	Nicholas Aaron
Speed	Lee Oakes
Shane	Paul Sharma
Finn	Charlie J Watts
Director	Terry Johnson
Designer	Annie Gosney
Lighting	Steve Barnett
Sound	Neil Alexander

Characters

Jake
Polly
Natasha
Carol
Russell
Buzz
Speed
Shane
Finn

The rooftop of a tower block in the East End of London. Many TV aerials and satellite dishes, a large puddle, discarded household furniture, piles of rubbish and various scattered detritus.

Some metal steps lead from the main larger area of roof up to a tiny platform. There's a doorway here, leading to the emergency stairs. This is the only entrance to the roof.

It is about 4.30 in the afternoon. Mid-September. Sunny.

Jake *enters. He is fourteen years old, slightly built and clutching a satchel. He is wearing a well-worn, but still clean and tidy, school uniform and glasses (the left lens is cracked and the bridge held together by sticky tape). His hair is neatly cut.*

Jake *makes his way down to main area of roof and sits in an old armchair. He is familiar and comfortable with these surroundings. It's a place he's been many times before – his secret hideaway.*

Jake *takes notebook from satchel and starts to read.*

He nods and murmurs thoughtfully.

Takes pen from pocket and writes.

Jake   Big … fish! Bigfish! … No, no.

Tears page from notebook and throws it aside.

Starts pacing the roof, continuing to write –

Glitter! Glitterpiranha! … No, no.

Polly *enters. She is fourteen years old and wearing the same school uniform as **Jake**, although hers is brand new (and has a skirt instead of trousers). Her hair is longish, but held primly in place by an elastic band. She is clutching a tiny tool box.*

Polly *watches **Jake** from the raised platform.*

Jake   Shark! Yes! Shark … glitter –

Jake *turns and sees **Polly**.*

He lets out a yelp of surprise and drops his notebook.

Loose pages flutter everywhere.

Polly   Oh, I'm sorry.

Jake *starts picking up pages.*

Polly *climbs down metal steps and starts helping him.*

Jake   Don't bother.

Polly   No bother.

Picks page from puddle.

This one's a bit soggy. Can't quite read –

Jake *snatched page from her.*

Jake   Don't! This is … it's *personal* stuff. You can't just stroll up here and start reading things willy-nilly! Watch out! You're treading on one now! You should be in a circus with feet that size. What you doing here anyway? This is *my* place! Go away!

Slight Pause.

Polly   I've only got three things to say to you. One: what I'm doing up here is none of your business. Two: the roof is not your private property – unless, of course, you have a special clause in your rent book, which I doubt. And three: I find it strange that someone who can write such magical words has such a spiteful tongue in his head … Now, I've got something I need to do, then I'll be gone. In the interim, I'd be grateful if you didn't speak to me again.

Goes to satellite dish on the edge of the roof.

She opens tool box and removes screwdriver.

She none too convincingly starts fiddling.

Pause.

Jake   Is it *really* magical?

Polly   … What?

Jake My writing.

Polly Bits.

Slight pause.

Jake I … I was wondering whose dish that was.

Slight pause.

I'm Jake.

Polly I know.

Jake How?

Polly Oh, please – Your eyes! Use them!

Indicates her school uniform.

Jake You go to my school!

Polly Started last week.

Jake Haven't seen you.

Polly Not surprised. All you do is hide between those two big dustbins at the back of the playground.

Jake I like it there.

Polly But, surely, they're a bit … well, smelly?

Jake Don't notice it after a few deep breaths.

Finn (*off stage*) AAARGHHNAAAHHH!

Polly *leans over ledge.*

Polly All right, Finn! Tell me when it gets better.

Finn (*off stage*) AAARGHHNAAAHH!

Polly *continues fiddling with satellite dish.*

Jake That … that voice! I've seen it – I mean, I've seen who it belongs to. He joined my class last week.

Polly That's my baby brother.

Jake   Baby! But … but he's huge! He grabbed two desks. One in each hand. And lifted them up. Above his head.

Polly   He's very strong for his age.

Jake   All the boys are scared of him. They call him the Monster –

Polly   He's *not* a monster! Everyone calls him that! Everywhere he goes! But he's not! He's very gentle! Cries easily, if you must know.

Finn   (*off stage*) AARGHHNAAAH!

Polly   (*calling*) OK, Finn! (*at* **Jake**) It's getting better.

Jake   You understand him?

Polly   It might sound like a meaningless groan to you but believe me – once you grasp the nuances, it's a very subtle form of communication.

Finn   (*off stage*) AARRGHHNAAAHHH!

Jake   Subtle? That?

Polly   Well, he's in a bad mood. The reception's gone fuzzy so he's missing his favourite programme. The one with real-life accidents. You know? Housewives setting themselves on fire with dodgy hairdryers –

Finn   (*off stage*) AAAH!

Polly   All right, Finn! – And everyone watches these programmes because they're supposed to be educational –

Jake   But all they really want to see is someone's head getting sliced off by helicopter blades.

Polly   Precisely.

Finn   (*off stage*) AAAH!

Polly   Thanks, Finn! – That's it! Picture's perfect. He'll quieten now.

Starts packing up tools etc.

We need a new dish really. Dad got this one on cheap somewhere. There was no instruction manual – You know anything about this sort of thing?

Jake   Haven't you've got to aim it at a satellite or something?

Points at the sky.

Polly   Perhaps I should put it higher – Oh!

Jake   What?

Polly   A dead bird … Poor thing. Only a baby. Must have fallen from one of the nests.

Peers closer at dead bird.

All mauve and scarlet. Little yellow beak. Come and have a look.

Jake   Rather not.

Polly   Can't hurt you.

Jake   Not that … I can be seen up there. By people in the football pitch.

Polly   There's no one in the football pitch.

Jake   But there might be. Any minute now. If he sees me – oh, you won't understand.

Polly   Try me.

Slight pause.

Jake   It's Russell –

Polly   The turbo-dreambabe?

Jake   Turbo *what*?

Polly   That's what's written all over the girls' toilets. TICK HERE IF YOU THINK RUSSELL'S A TURBO-DREAMBABE.

Jake   Bet the wall's covered.

Polly   *Everyone* loves him.

Jake   Love! I'll show you what your precious turbo-whatever has done … Come here! Come on!

Polly *goes to* **Jake**.

Jake   Feel!

Jake *points at top of his head.*

Polly *feels his head.*

Polly   Oooo …

Jake   An elbow did that.

Rolls trouser leg up.

And here!

Polly   Very colourful.

Jake   A foot! – And look in my eyes. Does the left one look a little bloodshot?

Polly   … Yes.

Jake   A fist!

Slight pause.

Polly   The turbo-dreambabe?

Jake   Bingo! – Hang on! You ticked! You *like* him!

Polly   I don't know if I *like* him –

Jake   But you *ticked*!

Polly   Yes, I ticked! The other day he took his shirt off in the playground and – yes, I admit – I felt a tingle.

Jake   Animal!

Slight pause.

Polly   I'm sorry you're bullied. Russell is a nasty piece of work. It's like my Mum said about Dad, 'Sometimes the worst presents come in the nicest wrapping paper.'

Slight pause.

Jake   Muscles! Who needs them? I don't want to do six thousand sit-ups a day. I don't care if I don't make people tingle –

Polly   But you do! At least … you do me.

Jake   … I do?

Polly   Your stories do.

Jake   How do you know about my stories?

Polly   The other day… when I was fixing up the satellite totally wrongly, I bet – I noticed …

Takes several folded sheets from pocket.

I'm sorry, I'm sorry. I know I shouldn't have. But … oh, Jake, there's such wonderful words here. When I read them I … I tingle as if a thousand Russells had revealed a thousand six-pack stomachs.

Slight pause.

Jake   You see the tower blocks? Over there! I imagine they're mountains! And other blocks – like this one – they can be castles. Or mountains. Depending on the story. And … those television aerials. They're a forest. I'm … I'm working on this new story. Don't know what it's about yet. But it'll have a dragon in it. A dragon with a head like … like a giant piranha. Or shark. And its skin is all shiny. It sparkles –

Polly   Like sequins!

Jake   Exactly! I'm trying to work out the dragon's name. I was thinking of something like … Glittershark.

Polly   Not quite right.

Slight pause.

Sharktwinkle!

Jake   No.

Natasha *enters. She's fifteen years old and, although she's wearing the same school uniform as* **Polly***, her skirt is much shorter, the shirt is bright pink and her shoes are stilettos. Her make-up is heavy and her hair, though not long, screams for attention. In place of a satchel, she has a handbag covered with sequins.*

Natasha *watches* **Jake** *and* **Polly***.*

Polly   Fishtwinkle – oh, no! That's terrible!

Polly *and* **Jake** *turn and see* **Natasha***.*

They let out a yelp of surprise.

Polly   Natasha! How did you get up here?

Natasha   How did I? – Oh, just my usual after-school abseiling. What d'you mean, how did I get here, you silly cow? I walked up the bloody stairs. The last two flights need a bloody government health warning. Thought the boys' toilets at school were bad enough.

Takes perfume from handbag and sprays herself.

Polly   How did you know I was up here?

Natasha   Your brother told me – Well, told's a bit of an exaggeration. 'Where's Polly, Finn?' 'Uggghh!' (*pointing up*) 'What? She's in her bedroom?' 'Uggghh!' (*pointing up*) Finally, I work out it's either heaven or the roof.

Takes lipstick and face compact from handbag and starts to retouch make-up.

And Polly – please don't take this the wrong way – but your brother stinks. The state of his hair should be punishable by law. And as for his breath! Ugh! It could strip nail varnish at twenty paces.

Starts to climb down stairs.

Polly   What you doing, Natasha?

Natasha   What's it look like – Oh, give us a hand, Pol.

Polly *helps* **Natasha** *down.*

Polly   You should wear sensible shoes.

Natasha   No girl wears shoes to be sensible.

Polly   They wear them to get blisters, do they?

Natasha   Beauty knows no pain – Now, Pol, quick. A word –

Natasha *pulls* **Polly** *to one side.*

Natasha   Looks like we've got a yellow alert situation here.

Polly   Yellow alert?

Natasha   Don't play dumb, Little Missy. Cast your mind back.
Your first day at school. You're standing alone in the playground.
You're close to tears –

Polly   I was not close to –

Natasha   Who saved you from total cred oblivion?

Polly   You made friends with me, if that's what you mean.

Natasha   And you know why? Because under your totally naff
surface, I detected the *real* you. The one who, by half-term, with
my help and a make-over –

Polly   I don't want a make-over –

Natasha   Park your lips! What did I tell you on that first day? Be
careful who you talk to. Ask me who's in, who's out. Did or did I
not say that?

Polly   You did.

Natasha   So why the geek?

Polly   He's *not* a geek! He's very nice.

Natasha   Orange alert! Niceness has nothing to do with it.
It's like saying someone with measles is nice. It don't matter.
Geekiness is contagious! Now, let's get away from here pronto –

Polly   I *like* Jake.

Natasha   Red alert! Pol, you'll be hiding between the dustbins before the term's out.

Polly   I don't care! He's my friend. And if you can't accept that, then … well, you're not the deep, warm, sensitive, mature person I thought you were. Someone who's as beautiful inside as she is out.

Slight pause.

Natasha   … Hello, Jake.

Slight pause.

I'm doing my hair different now. Had it cut since last term.

Polly   Don't talk about yourself. Be interested in *him.*

Slight pause.

Natasha   So, Jake … What do *you* think about my hair?

Polly   I didn't mean that!

Jake   Looked better before.

Natasha *stares at* **Jake**.

Jake   Your hair. When it was longer. Really suited you.

Polly   Jake, I don't think you should –

Natasha   Let him finish.

Slight pause.

Jake   Everyday you'd do it slightly different. Sometimes swept this way. Sometimes that. And no matter what style it always looked … oh, so perfect. A real work of art. The effort that went into that.

Natasha   Hours, believe me.

Jake   And you wore hairclips – My favorite! The one with yellow flowers.

Natasha   *My* favorite too. I've still got it.

Searches in handbag.

Jake   But shorter… it's like you've lost part of you. Even your make-up looks different.

Polly   Stop flirting.

Natasha   He's not flirting. He's talking like one of the girls. What's more, he's the only one who's had the guts to be honest. My hair was better longer –

Finds hairclip.

Jake?

Jake   That's the one.

Natasha   Won't suit me now – You have it, Pol.

Polly   … Me?

Jake   It'd suit you.

Natasha   The voice of an expert.

Gives hairclip to **Polly**.

Polly   Tasha, you know I can't…

Natasha   There's nothing wrong with making the most of yourself, Pol.

Polly *gazes at hairclip.*

Natasha   You've got to … express yourself now and then. Not bottle everything up. Otherwise … you're gonna explode.

Jake   It's just a hairclip.

Polly   Try telling my dad that.

Natasha   Dads! Dads! Dads! What've I told you, Pol? You mustn't let it bother you. Water off a duck's back. Just like mine.

Jake   What's wrong with *your* dad?

Slight pause.

Natasha   … Hardly says a word to me.

Jake   Why?

Natasha   Just doesn't ... like me any more, I guess. If I walk in the room he looks right through me. Or worse – like I've got a dog turd smeared across my forehead. Oh, I know what he's thinking. What he thinks of me – You know, I was in hospital last term. Just before the summer holidays. A whole week. Guess how many times Dad visited.

Slight pause.

Spilt milk. Been there. Seen it. Boohooed that!

Carol *enters. She is fourteen years old and, although she's wearing her school uniform in the same way as* **Natasha** *– short skirt, coloured shirt (lemon), stilettos, gold handbag etc. – she can't quite pull it off. Nothing seems to fit her properly and, even if it did, the awkwardness and self-consciousness would still remain.*

Carol's *a little breathless and clings to the rail for support.*

Natasha   Carol! I thought I told you to wait downstairs, Little Missy.

Carol   Didn't say. Wait a million. Years though. Did you? Honestly, Pol, I can put up. With your brother breathing last night's curry. I can even put up with his Richter scale farts. But when he starts setting fire to them – well, I'm outa there. What you doing up here anyway?

Notices **Jake**.

Carol   Yellow alert! – Geek!

Polly   Don't call him that!

Carol   Orange alert!

Polly   He's my friend!

Carol   Red alert!

Natasha   And mine!

Slight pause.

Carol *starts to negotiate descending the steps.*

Natasha   Leave us alone, Carol.

Polly   Perhaps we should all go.

Natasha   Don't you dare, Polly. I was just beginning to enjoy myself – Carol, sling your bloody hook!

Carol   *I* was your friend first! Before *her*! Help me down.

Slight pause.

Don't leave me out.

Natasha   Clear off!

Carol *starts to cry.*

Slight pause.

Jake *goes to* **Carol**.

He helps her down.

Natasha   On your head be it, Jake.

Carol *has now reached the roof.*

She smiles briefly at Jake, then starts strolling round.

Natasha   The level of conversation's gonna drop faster than Carol's knickers in the boys' toilets.

Carol   Why you such a bloody bitch all the time?

Natasha   You *make* me! Bloody following me everywhere. Everything I do, you copy. You bloody wannabe. I buy stilettos, so do you –

Carol   You didn't bloody invent stilettos!

Natasha   (*indicating handbag*) I buy this. The very next day – Oh, surprise, surprise –

Carol   They were in a sale!

Natasha   I wear a coloured shirt –

Carol   Mine's citrus lemon!

Natasha   Because they ran out of frosty pink. You even cut your hair 'cos I did.

Carol   I was thinking of this for ages!

Natasha   Liar!

Carol   Tell me this, Miss All That. If you're so bloody special, why did Shane dump you?

Natasha   Shane did *not* dump me.

Polly   Who's Shane?

Jake   He left school last year – Why *did* Shane dump you?

Natasha   He didn't. *I* dumped *him*.

Carol   Then why the Richter scale eight boohoos?

Natasha   The boohoos weren't for Shane.

Carol   Not what you told me.

Natasha   Think I'd tell you the truth, Little Miss Internet?

Jake   Why would you dump someone like Shane? He's so … you know.

Natasha   Oh, yes, I know. Shane the Brooding. Shane the Cool. Shane the Let's-Paint-My-Bedroom-Black. Shane the Let's-Stick-A-Compass-in-My-Palm-Whenever-I'm-Fed-Up. Oh, honestly! Sound like me?

Carol   You said you *loved* it.

Natasha   Boyfriend stuff is complicated. You won't understand till you get one.

Carol   I've *got* a boyfriend!

Natasha   One kiss from Russell is *not* having a boyfriend.

Carol   He can't take his eyes off me.

Natasha   For chrissakes, Carol, don't you know anything?
Listen, if you go to a party, you wanna know what boy fancies
you? I mean, really, *really* fancies you? It's the one *not* looking at
you. 'Can't keep his eyes off me!' – Jesus! Shall I tell you what
your precious Russell told wonderful, brooding Shane kissing you
was? Charity!

Carol   Liar!

Natasha   Ask him yourself.

Carol   I will!

Leans over edge of roof.

Russell!

Jake   Don't!

Natasha   She's joking.

Carol   (*calling*) Up here! With Natasha!

Jake   She's not! He plays down there!

Polly   The football pitch!

Carol   He's coming!

Polly   Hide, Jake.

Carol   (*at Natasha*) And he's not alone.

Jake *starts looking for a hiding place.*

Natasha   Buzz and Speed are always with him.

Carol   Not just Buzz and Speed.

Natasha   … Shane?

Carol *laughs excitedly.*

Jake *is unable to find hiding place.*

Polly   Behind me! Quick!

Jake *gets behind* **Polly**.

Natasha   Oh, my God! Polly! It's Shane!

Polly   Tasha, we need your help. Quick!

Natasha   … What?

Polly   We need to hide Jake. Russell will –

Jake   Kill me!

Natasha   (*at Carol*) This is all your bloody fault, Little Missy.

Polly   Quick!

Natasha *runs to stand beside* **Polly**.

Polly   Closer, Tasha!

Carol   What's going on??

Polly   Carol, we need you too. Quick! Or do you want to see Jake hurt?

Carol   Hurt?

Polly   Hurry!

Carol *rushes to join* **Polly** *and* **Natasha**.

Jake *hides behind them.*

Polly   Close up, Carol. No gaps!

Russell *enters. He is fifteen years old and glossily good-looking. His school uniform has been reduced to trousers and shirt, the latter mostly unbuttoned and with the sleeves rolled up. Instead of shoes, he's wearing trainers.*

Russell   (*in a voice of a sports commentator*) 'The winner! Russell the Love Muscle adds Gold Medal for Tower Block Climbing to his long list of trophies. Is there any stopping this sex-machine, babe-magnet?'

Calls down stairs.

Come on, you two. Hear them panting down there? Pathetic. But, girls, feast your eyes! Am I breathless?

Girls   … No.

Russell   Sweating?

Girls   … No.

Russell   Tired?

Girls   … No.

Russell   Do not adjust your sets, girls. You are witnessing perfection. Look at you! Too dazzled to move. 'The crowd cheers at this spunky, funky, hard-bod hunky. Women are throwing flowers. He blows one a kiss! She faints –'

Buzz *and* **Speed** *enter. They are fourteen years old and wearing the reduced school uniform favored by* **Russell**, *although their shirts are not unbuttoned. They are both shorter than* **Russell** *and lack the arrogant dazzle that makes* **Russell** *their natural leader.*

They are carrying sports bags instead of satchels.

Buzz *is carrying an extra one which, presumably, belongs to* **Russell**.

Both of them are out of breath and look close to collapse.

Russell   Talk about fainting! Pathetic or what? Ha!

Buzz   He kept pushing me, Russ.

Speed   He got in the way, Russ.

Buzz   I'm carrying your bag, Russ.

Speed   He used it to trip me, Russ.

Russell   Out of the way, losers – time to greet the fans.

Jumps to main area of roof.

I know what you're thinking, girls. Why can't my hair shine like his? And as for his eyelashes – they're wasted on a bloke! Don't blame me. I was born with these gifts …Others – I worked at!

Lifts shirt to reveal stomach.

Carol *lets out an involuntary squeal.*

Russell   Know what these muscles are called?

Slight pause.

Horny as hell!

Buzz *and* **Speed** *go to descend the metal stairs.*

Russell   You two! Jump like me! A man!

Buzz *and* **Speed** *stand on edge of raised area.*

They're psyching themselves to jump, visibly nervous.

Russell   Hey, Natasha. All right?

Natasha   Fine.

Russell   Avoiding us lately?

Natasha   Why should I?

Russell   Our Shane-boy.

Natasha   Ancient history.

Russell   Exactly what I just said. When Shane heard what's-her-face call you were up here. 'Come up,' I said. 'Let bygones be bygones. So you split up! No big deal. You can't avoid each other for the rest of your lives. Right?'

At **Buzz** *and* **Speed**.

Jump, you two!

Buzz   Stop calling us 'you two'!

Speed   We've got names.

Shane *enters and, without missing a beat, pushes* **Buzz** *and* **Speed**. *They fall awkwardly to the lower level.*

Polly, **Natasha** *and* **Carol** *gasp.*

Russell *bursts out laughing.*

Shane *is sixteen years old and wearing black leather trousers, boots, red silk shirt – unbuttoned to reveal a silver neckchain – black jacket and sunglasses. His hair is longish and well groomed.*

Russell   Nice one, Shane!

Buzz   Bloody stupid, that!

Speed   Could've broken my neck!

Russell   Shut up, you two!

Shane *sits at top of metal steps.*

Slight pause.

Natasha   Hello, Shane.

Slight pause.

How's it going?

Slight pause.

Have a good summer?

Shane *still doesn't respond.*

Carol   Russell! When you kissed me. Remember?

Russell   No.

Carol   Yes, you do.

Russell   If you say so.

Carol   Natasha said that … well, said you said. Said you said to Shane –

Russell   Said *what*, for chrissakes?

Carol   Said … it was charity.

Buzz *and* **Speed** *start laughing.*

Stop it! Stop it!

Natasha   Belt up, you scrotums!

Buzz *and* **Speed** *stop laughing.*

Russell   Well, to be honest with you – what's your name again?

Natasha   Carol. Her name's Carol.

Russell   Well, Carol, it's probably true. But let me explain! I am a dreamboat. You are not. Now, when a dreamboat kisses a dreamboat-challenged person – it's always charity. This is not a bad thing. I'm giving you something that – in normal circumstances – you wouldn't stand a hope in hell of getting. Don't tell me you didn't like the kiss.

Carol   … No. I mean, yes!

Russell   Would you like another smackeroonie?

Natasha   Control yourself. Carol.

Russell   Come here.

Polly   Don't move.

Carol *is whimpering at the back of her throat.*

Russell   Oh, Carol! Let me kiss you…Let me kiss you…

Suddenly, **Carol** *can resist no more and rushes at* **Russell***.*

Immediately, **Buzz** *and* **Speed** *get a glimpse of* **Jake***.*

Buzz   Geek alert!

Speed   Geek alert!

Russell   What? Where?

Turns away from **Carol** *before kissing.*

Russell   Well, well, well, hiding behind the girls. How pathetic. How … one hundred per cent geek!

Carol   Where's my kiss?

Russell   Get him, you two!

Buzz *and* **Speed** *go to grab* **Jake***.*

Jake *runs.*

Buzz *and* **Speed** *chase.*

Jake   Help!

Polly   Leave him!

Natasha   Don't, Russ!

Carol   Where's my bloody kiss?

Buzz *and* **Speed** *catch* **Jake**.

Jake   Help!

Buzz   Kick him, Russ!

Speed   Punch him, Russ!

Russell   I've got a better idea. Let's dangle him over the edge.

Buzz   Wicked!

Speed   Awesome!

Jake   Polly!

Buzz *and* **Speed** *take* **Jake** *to edge of roof.*

Polly   He's done anything to you!

Jake   Natasha! Help!

Natasha   Stop it, Russ! Stop! Shane – tell him!

Carol   My kiss!

Russell   Shut up about your bloody kiss!

Jake   Carol! Help me!

Carol   Let him go!

Russell   Hey, Shane! You should see the geek's face! All scared and – He's pulling Buzz's hair! Ha! A geek with cheek!

Speed   He's pulling *my* hair!

Buzz   I'm Buzz.

Speed   I'm Speed.

Russell   Don't get touchy now, you two – Dangle him!

Jake   NOOOOO!

Polly   Stop!

Carol   Stop!

Natasha   You're gonna really hurt him.

Russell   I'm trying my best, yeah.

Polly   What if they *drop* him?

Russell   Then he'll go splat!

Russell, **Buzz** *and* **Speed** *laugh.*

Natasha   Shane!

Polly   You can't dangle him! Please! He … he was telling us a story – Wasn't he, Tasha?

Natasha   … What? Oh … yeah! He was telling us a story.

Russell   So what.

Polly   We want to know the end – Don't we?

Natasha   Yes.

Carol   Yes.

Russell   I hate stories.

Jake   Help! Help!

Natasha   Shane! Tell him! *Please!*

Slight pause.

Russell   What's it to be, Shane? Dangle or story?

Shane *looks at* **Natasha**.

She stares at him.

Shane   … Story.

Russell   But, Shane –

Natasha   You heard!

Slight pause.

Buzz *and* **Speed** *stand* **Jake** *safely back on roof.*

They let go of him.

Pause.

Russell   So?

Pause.

Polly   It … It was about this Princess, wasn't it, Jake? Am I
right? Yes? This Princess. What happened, Jake?

Slight pause.

That's right! Yes! She lived in a Castle. Well, I suppose *all*
Princesses live in *Castles*, don't they?

Natasha   Wouldn't be seen without one.

Carol   No way.

Slight pause.

Polly   And this Princess … she lived in a Castle with her Dad.

Natasha   He's the King, right?

Polly   Exactly, Natasha! Thank you for reminding me. The
Princess lived in a Castle with her dad who was indeed the King.

Russell   Bloody riveting this! – Now, don't tell me. Her mum
was, indeed, the Queen.

Polly   No. The Princess didn't have a mother. She died –

Russell   At childbirth! Boring! – Shane! Let's dangle the geek!
He's not even telling it.

Natasha   The Queen had been murdered, if you must know.

Slight pause.

Very nastily.

Slight pause.

Horribly.

Buzz   … How?

Polly   One day … the Castle was attacked. By the King's enemies. The Kingdom had been at war for a long time.

Speed   The King should have been prepared then.

Polly   Well … yes. He was. Usually. The King was a great soldier.

Buzz   So how come the enemy surprised him?

Natasha   … The baby Princess.

Carol   The Castle was celebrating. Right?

Polly   Exactly right, Carol. It was the day for celebrating the birth of the Princess! A holiday for everyone. The Castle was full of food and music and flowers.

Buzz   A good ol' booze-up.

Speed   Peanuts and sausages on sticks.

Carol   Everyone strutting their funky stuff.

Natasha   And that's when the enemy attacked!

Buzz   Bet the Castle was slaughtered.

Polly   The King was too good a soldier for that. In fact, the King defeated the enemy that day!

Buzz   But the Queen!

Speed   What happened to her?

Russell   Yeah. You said it was something nasty.

Buzz and **Speed**   Yeah.

Polly   She was…shot in the heart with a single arrow.

Russell, **Buzz** *and* **Speed** *are not impressed.*

Polly   And then ... her head was chopped off.

They are still unimpressed.

Polly   And then ... her head was eaten by a hungry pig.

Buzz, Speed and **Russell**   Wicked!

Carol   I feel a bit sick.

Polly   After that ... the King never let his defenses down again. Am I getting this right, Jake? The King banned pleasure from the Castle. No dancing. No singing.

Natasha   No flowers.

Polly   Nothing pretty or frivolous at all. He thought these things would turn the Princess weak.

Russell   (to **Buzz** *and* **Speed**) Like you two

Polly   And, as the Princess had to rule after him one day, and possibly fight many battles, he had to train her to be strong – Right, Jake?

Jake *nods and murmurs.*

...The King made the Princess wear a simple dress. And only one colour ... black!

Carol   Not even citrus lemon?

Polly   No.

Natasha   Bet her shoes were sensible too.

Polly   *Very* sensible. And guess what she had to drink ... Vinegar!

Buzz   Disgusting!

Polly   And eat ... Plain bread!

Speed   No butter?

Polly   No.

Buzz   What about margarine?

Polly   No! Nothing! The King forbade it! And then, one night …

Jake *thumps floor.*

Polly   What? A thump … ? Yes! That's it! I remember now!
Thank you, Jake. The Princess heard something thump against her
window.

Buzz   What is it?

Polly   A bird.

Speed   Is it dead?

Polly   Its neck's broken.

Carol   The Princess buries it!

Polly   In a secret corner of the Castle.

Buzz   Why do girls bury things?

Speed   Instead of cutting them up?

Jake   … There's something *inside* the bird.

Polly   What, Jake?

Buzz   Yeah, what?

Speed   What?

Carol   What?

Jake   … A flower seed.

Polly   Of course. That's what the bird ate for dinner. So when
the bird is buried – the seed grows! And the next summer a flower
appears and the Princess picks it and –

Has taken hairclip from her pocket.

Look! I'm going to wear it in my hair.

Buzz   Don't let the King see.

Polly   Too late!

Carol   Yellow alert.

Polly   The Princess says, 'I'm sorry, Dad! Please! It's just a flower. Please – Ahhh!'

Speed   What's happened?

Polly   He's … he's hit me.

Russell   Bully!

Polly   'What's that, Dad? Oh, no! No!'

Carol   What's he say?

Buzz   What?

Speed   What?

Polly   He thinks I'm weak and frivolous.

Natasha   No!

Polly   He doesn't want a daughter like me.

Jake   You're banished!

Slight pause.

Polly   …I leave the Castle.

Walks around roof.

And for a while … there's nothing. I don't know where I'm going. Just … a wasteland. I walk and walk. And then – yes! – I find a forest!

Jake   She plants her flower.

Polly   The flower is full of lots of seeds.

Buries hairclip beneath some rubbish.

Jake   And one year later …

Polly   Hundreds of flowers!

Jake   The following year!

Polly   Thousands!

Jake   The next!

Polly   Millions! Look at them! Millions of yellow flowers! As far as the eye can see! So beautiful. And I'm … I'm so happy here in the forest of a million yellow flowers. Smell them! And, what's that? There! Look! In the lake!

Points at puddle.

Dolphins! Splashing and playing together. Oh, yes! Oh, yes! Yes!

Jake   … And then, one day, a Prince arrives.

Buzz   Me!

Speed   No! Me!

Jake   The Prince is the most handsome man in all the land.

Russell   Someone call my name?

Buzz   *I* said it first.

Speed   No! *I* did!

Russell   Shut it, you two!

Jake *gets the supermarket trolley.*

He wheels it in front of **Russell**.

Jake   The Prince rode a chariot.

Russell   You must be bloody joking!

Jake   Said the Prince. Because he was strong and proud. He thought he should walk everywhere. But he also knew that riding in … the solid gold chariot was an honour. An honour only given to true heroes.

Slight pause.

Russell *gets in supermarket trolley.*

Russell   Where's my horses then?

Everyone looks at **Buzz** *and* **Speed**.

Buzz   No way!

Speed   No way!

Russell   Shane?

Slight pause.

Shane *points at supermarket trolley.*

Buzz *and* **Speed** *grab hold of it.*

Russell   Gee up, Lightning! Gee up, Ned!

Buzz   Hang on a bloody minute! Who's Ned?

Russell   You are.

Buzz   Oh, no! If he's Lightning, I am *not* going to be called Ned. You can stuff that up your –

Jake   Thunder!

Slight pause.

Russell   Gee up, Thunder and Lightning!

Buzz *and* **Speed** *pull supermarket trolley.*

Russell   Faster! Faster! Come on, you two!

Buzz *and* **Speed** *pull supermarket trolley round.*

Russell   Faster! Faster!

Buzz *and* **Speed** *pull supermarket trolley faster.*

Russell   Faster!

Speed   That's it! I've had enough!

Jake   The horses were exhausted so the Prince – who was as kind and understanding as he was handsome – let them rest by a lake in the middle of a forest.

Buzz *and* **Speed** *pull supermarket trolley to puddle.*

Polly   Who are you?

Speed   Lightning!

Russell   She's *not* talking to you! You're a bloody horse – Hello! I'm a Prince.

Polly   Beautiful.

Russell   I work out.

Polly   Not you. My forest. Look! A million yellow flowers.

Jake   But, as far as the Prince was concerned, the Princess was more beautiful than all the flowers put together.

Slight pause.

Polly   Why are you looking at me like that?

Russell   … Like what?

Polly   Like there's something you want to say.

Pause.

Oh, I know it's difficult. For a Prince like you, I mean. To say things … gentle things. You've had to be strong and brave all your life. As hard as your six-pack stomach. But you can say them to me, you know.

Slight pause.

Do you think I'm beautiful?

Russell   … Not bad.

Polly   Do you want me to leave my forest and live with you in your Castle?

Russell   … I'm easy.

Slight pause.

All right. Yeah. I wouldn't mind.

Polly   But, Prince, my forest is so beautiful. How can I leave it? Even for a Love Muscle like you?

Russell   You're … you're playing games with me now! I never liked you in the first place – Shane!

Polly   Don't go!

Jake   The Princess could see the Prince was upset. She knew he didn't mean what he was saying –

Russell   I bloody do!

Jake   So she offered him a challenge.

Slight pause.

Polly   Prince! There is … something inside me that tingles for you. Honestly. I can't explain it. I'd like to give you chance – or me a chance…If you can find me something more beautiful than a million yellow flowers. If you can do that, I will follow you anywhere.

Jake   So the Prince searched.

Russell *looks at* **Shane**.

Shane *indicates* **Russell** *should search.*

Russell *searches roof.*

He finds an old shoe and takes it to **Polly**.

Polly   The most beautiful shoe ever made. Decorated with rubies and diamonds and stitched with gold thread … Beautiful. But not beautiful enough.

Slight pause.

Russell *throws shoe aside.*

He searches roof once more.

He finds an old baseball cap and takes it to **Polly**.

Russell   This is a crown! Right? It's made of platinum. It's decorated with a trillion bloody diamonds. Beautiful or what?

Polly   Beautiful. But not beautiful enough.

Russell *throws the cap angrily.*

Buzz   Go to a Witch.

Speed   Yeah! Wicked! Ask a Witch.

All look at **Natasha**.

Natasha   Well, that's bloody typical!

Slight pause.

Come on, then. What you waiting for?

Russell *goes to* **Natasha**.

Natasha   Hello, Prince. So you've got to find –

Russell   I haven't told you yet!

Natasha   I'm a bloody Witch, dickhead!

Slight pause.

So … Little Miss Flower Power wants you to find something more beautiful than a million yellow flowers. I can do that. But first … you have got to pay.

Russell   How much?

Natasha   Not money, you turbo-dreambabe. A kiss.

Russell   What? Here? In front of … everyone?

Natasha   But we're in my own witchy hovel.

Russell *looks at* **Shane**, *then back at* **Natasha**.

Natasha   I'm waiting.

Russell *kisses* **Natasha**.

It grows increasingly passionate.

Carol *slaps at* **Russell**.

Carol   Stop it, stop it!

Russell   Hey! What's your problem?

Carol   Kiss *me*. It's not fair –

Natasha   Calm down! Jesus! Get a grip!

Carol *calms.*

Natasha   You make yourself look a bloody idiot sometimes. Then you wonder why everyone's laughing. It's humiliating. You should be bloody ashamed of yourself. Hear me? Ashamed.

Slight pause.

You'll have to forgive my little creature, Prince.

Russell   Little creature?

Natasha   … My pet frog.

Slight pause.

Carol   … Croak, croak.

Natasha   And now, Prince. I'll grant your wish.

Takes spray from handbag.

This is my most magic potion. One spray of this and the Princess will swoon. She'll forget all about wanting something more beautiful than a million yellow flowers. Because all she'll want is you!

Sprays perfume on **Russell***.*

Russell   Stop!

Natasha   Done now!

Buzz *and* **Speed** *laugh.*

Russell   It's the knacker's yard for you two!

Polly   Ooo! What's that swoon inducing smell?

Slight pause.

Russell *goes to* **Polly***.*

Polly   Very, *very* swoony. But … a bit too fruity for my taste.

Russell   That's it! I've had enough!

Shane   You shouldn't have trusted the Witch.

Russell   *You* did!

Shane   Her magic potion worked then –

Jake   Said the Wizard.

Pause.

Shane   … Let me tell you about the Witch.

Slight pause.

A million years ago I met her. On a planet far away. She was a powerful sorceress then. Her magic potion was the most potent in the universe. Savage monsters could be tamed with one whiff. *I* was tamed.

Slight pause.

And then, one day, she refused to answer when I called her name. I screamed so loud stars became supernova.

Slight pause.

She has spent a million years avoiding me. Fleeing each planet as I arrive. I couldn't worked out why she loved me so much one day … then, the next, not at all. But I thought about it and thought about it. And the only conclusion I could come to was…an egg.

Natasha   Wh … what?

Shane   A Dragon's egg, of course.

Buzz   Wicked!

Speed   Awesome!

Carol   What about the egg?

Jake   … The Wizard told the Prince about this Dragon. It lives in the mountain –

Polly   I've heard about this Dragon. It's got jaws like a shark.

Jake   And scales like sequins.

Polly   And this Dragon – yes, of course! – it lays eggs.

Jake and **Polly**   Eggs more beautiful than a million yellow flowers!

Slight pause.

Shane   Go to the mountains. Find the Dragon's egg. The Princess will be yours.

Buzz   But … won't there be two Dragons.

Speed   A Mummy and a Daddy?

Jake   It's an hermaphrodite Dragon.

Slight pause.

Half boy, half girl.

Russell   Relative of yours, Jake?

Jake   It's a ferocious Dragon. It might be covered with sequins. But each sequin is as sharp as a razor blade. So be careful, Prince. Be very careful.

Slight pause.

Russell   (*in sports commentator voice*) 'The Prince faces the challenge without fear. Is this the bravest man on earth or what? In a few incredible strides he scales the heights of the mountain.'

Climbs metal stairs.

'It's freezing cold, but is the Prince shivering? No! He's not even wearing protective clothing. Is this man mortal we have to ask ourselves. And there … Is it? Yes! I believe it is! He's found it! Easy!'

Takes football from his sports bag.

The Dragon's egg!

Shane   The cold must be making the Prince hallucinate.

Russell *stares at* **Shane**.

Russell   It's not the – ?

Shane *shakes his head.*

Russell   'Undeterred, the turbo-dreamboat of a Prince searches
again! What stamina! What grit! And now – Yes!'

Lifts an old lampshade in air.

The Dragon's egg!

Shane *shakes his head.*

Russell   *What* then, for chrissakes?

Carol   I'll help you! Yeah, me, the frog! You see, ever since
you came to visit the Witch … I've been thinking about you.
Richter scale eight crush. Can't help it. Don't understand it –
Before you say anything, I don't want a kiss. You don't fancy
frogs. That's your problem. No reason to hate you. I'll find a frog
of my own to snog when this is over. In the meantime, there's the
egg.

She points.

Russell   Where?

Carol   There!

Russell   But what? *Where*?

Pause.

Ah! I get it! Imagination. Okay, okay …I see it! There! More
beautiful than anything I ever thought I'd find.

Shane   Describe it.

Russell   Well….it's in a nest. A huge nest. Whole branches
instead of twigs. All twisted and broken together – How's that?

Shane   Pretty good. Go on.

Slight pause.

Russell   The egg's in the middle of the nest. It's very big!
Sparkling with a million colours ... I'm climbing into the nest
now ... Insects buzz all round me ... Wood cracks at my feet ...

Picks up the imaginary egg.

The Princess will be mine!

Natasha   You helped him find it, you frog!

Carol   You *made* me a frog! With the last Witch I served I was
a cat! A sleek, graceful cat with big green eyes. Yes, I change
depending on who I'm with. But it's the Witch that changes me.
You hear that? I don't change myself. I hate you for changing me
into a frog. I hate you for laughing because someone ... someone I
love thinks I'm ugly.

Russell   I don't think you're ugly.

Carol   Then why didn't you kiss me?

Russell   Because I don't feel ... like that towards you. Doesn't
mean I think you're ugly. We can still be...you know.

Carol   What?

Russell   You know.

Carol   No. What?

Russell   ... Well, we don't have to be enemies.

Slight pause.

Jake   And look! You're not a frog any more. You're a beautiful
nightingale.

Carol   A nightingale! – Princess! Look what the Prince has
found!

Russell   The Dragon's egg!

Polly   It's more beautiful than a million yellow flowers! Prince,
take me to your Castle.

Jake   And the Prince and Princess were married!

Polly *and* **Russell** *parade hand in hand.*

Everyone, except **Natasha**, *cheers and claps.*

Buzz *and* **Speed** *tear bits of paper up and throw them as confetti.*

Natasha   It's not over!

The celebration dies down.

Natasha   You think it's that bloody easy. Eh? Find a beautiful egg and all live happily ever after – You make me puke!

Shane   … What're you going to do?

Slight pause.

Natasha   Curse the egg!

Russell   What curse?

Natasha   The egg's beauty! It'll be too much for the Princess! It'll hypnotize her. Possess her! Yes!

Looks at **Polly**.

Natasha   Do it!

Slight pause.

Do it!

Polly *stares in front of her.*

Polly   Oh, the colours! The lights! The shapes!

Russell *goes to* **Shane**.

Russell   I've got a feeling that Witch has cursed the egg.

Shane   I think you're right.

Russell   You're a bloody Wizard. Break the spell.

Shane   It's too powerful for me.

Russell   What now?

Shane   Does the Princess love you?

Russell   Who knows?

Shane   Do *you* love *her*?

Russell   I ... well ...

Shane   *Could* you love her?

Russell   ... Probably.

Shane   Then you must go to her. Every day. Tell her how much she means to you. Perhaps, in time, she will love you back. And – who knows? – this love might break the spell.

Russell   You don't sound too sure.

Shane   I'm not.

Slight pause.

Russell *goes to* **Polly**.

Russell   Hello, Princess. You know, I've been thinking about you ... a lot. You know? In my mind! You pop into it.

Slight pause.

I've never spoken to anyone like this before –

Buzz *and* **Speed** *giggle.*

Shut up, you two. This is important. Help or clear off!

Buzz   Sorry.

Speed   Sorry.

Slight pause.

Russell   I've seen lots of nasty things, Princess. In battles. You know? It's hard out there. Tough. I've seen friends really hurt. You know what I'm saying? Out there – I've done what ... what a Prince had to do. Otherwise ... well, he'll never be King.

Slight pause.

Princess ... please ... listen to me. I'm trying ...

Polly   Oh, Prince.

Jake   It's cracking!

Shane   The egg!

Polly   It mustn't hatch! Nothing must damage that beautiful shell!

Picks up imaginary egg and starts to run.

Russell, **Buzz** *and* **Speed** *chase after her.*

Everyone is crying out, adding to the general pandemonium.

Jake   Catch her!

Russell   Stop!

Shane   Don't panic!

Buzz   It's all right!

Speed   Don't worry!

Polly   The egg mustn't break!

Buzz   Princess!

Speed   Careful!

Jake   Mind the edge!

Polly *is standing by the satellite dish now.*

Polly   I hate you! Hate what you've done to my beautiful egg! You monster! Hate you!

Buzz   Who's she talking to?

Speed   The baby Dragon.

Carol   It's hatched.

Buzz   It's broken the shell.

Jake   The Dragon's at her feet.

Shane   She's going to kill it!

Natasha   No!

Russell   No!

Carol   No!

Buzz   No!

Speed   No!

Natasha *rushes to* **Shane**.

Natasha   Shane! Don't let her! Please! I never meant this to happen! If I could go back and change the story, I would. *Believe* me. I *would*.

Polly *screams out and violently stamps her foot.*

Silence.

Long pause.

Natasha   Wh … what have you done?

Slight pause.

Slowly, **Natasha** *goes to* **Polly**.

She sees the dead bird.

Natasha   It's dead!

Falls against satellite dish.

Shane *rushes to* **Natasha**.

Shane   Tasha!

Finn   (*offstage*) AHHHHHHHHGHH!

Everyone freezes.

Slight pause.

Russell   What's that?

Buzz   That noise.

Speed   I think it's –

Buzz   It is!

Russell   Can't be!

Carol   It is!

Buzz and **Speed**   Him!

Russell   Run!

Russell, **Buzz** and **Speed** *explode in activity and scarper for stairs as –*

Finn enters. He is fifteen years old and very large, in all directions, for his age. He is wearing well-worn black jeans, boots and a T-shirt emblazoned with some heavy-metal logo, many silver rings and studded wristbands. His hair is extremely long and – like the rest of him – in need of a wash.

Finn   WAAAAAGOOOOOAAAH!

Russell, **Buzz** and **Speed** *yelp and scarper.*

Russell   The Monster!

Buzz   The Monster!

Speed   The Monster!

Russell, **Buzz** and **Speed** *hide.*

Polly   Don't call him that! You'll upset him! – It's all right, Finn.

Finn   WAAAAGOOOOOAAAH!

Polly   Shhh! Don't worry, Finn. I'll explain.

Polly *whispers in* **Finn***'s ear.*

She points at **Jake***.*

Jake *gasps.*

Finn *murmurs and nods.*

Polly *continues whispering in* **Finn***'s ear.*

She points at **Natasha**.

Natasha *gasps*.

Finn *murmurs and nods*.

Polly *continues whispering in* **Finn**'s *ear*.

She points at **Carol**.

Carol *gasps*.

Finn *murmurs and nods*.

Polly *continues whispering in* **Finn**'s *ear*.

She points at **Russell**.

Russell *cries out*.

Finn *murmurs and nods*.

Polly *continues whispering in* **Finn**'s *ear*.

She points at **Buzz** *and* **Speed**.

They both yell.

Finn *murmurs and nods*.

Polly *continues whispering in* **Finn**'s *ear*.

She points at **Shane**.

Finn *murmurs and nods*.

Polly *points at herself*.

Finn's *nodding and murmuring get more emphatic*.

Polly *points at dead bird*.

Finn's *nodding and murmuring get even more emphatic*.

Polly *points at* **Finn**.

Finn *nods and cries out gleefully and grabs hold of* **Polly**.

Polly   The Dragon who laid the egg! Help!

Russell   The Dragon who laid the egg?!

Buzz and **Speed**   Him!?

Polly   Show them, Finn?

Finn *claws his hands and roars.*

Finn   RAAAAAGGGHHHHH!

All   THE DRAGON!

Polly   Help! Help! I've killed what was in the Dragon's egg. Now the Dragon's kidnapped me for revenge. He's taken me to the top of the mountain. Help! Help!

Natasha   It's all my fault!

Russell   No mine!

Carol   No mine!

Jake   Mine!

Buzz   How's it *your* fault?

Speed   Who are you in all this anyway?

Jake   I'm … her father.

Russell   The King!

Carol   The one who wouldn't let out a flower in her hair.

Buzz   The one who banished her.

Jake   That's me!

Speed   Then it *is* your fault!

Russell   Where you been all this bloody time?

Jake   After what I did to my daughter … I realized I was wrong. I … I was so upset. I hid. Wouldn't show my face. Thought no one would want to see my face anyway. But then … then I realized. That wasn't the answer. It just made the problem worse. So now … now I'm not hiding any more. I'm here to save my daughter.

Save her from the Dragon. Is there anyone brave enough to help me?

Russell   I will.

Buzz   Me too.

Speed   And me.

Natasha   And me.

Shane   And me.

Carol   And me!

Buzz   What can you do?

Speed   You're a bloody nightingale.

Natasha   Not any more she's not! Like the King, I'm sorry for what I've done. I've been a bit of a cow really. Let's be friends again – I make you human and beautiful!

Buzz   What about me?

Speed   And me.

Shane   You too! Human! Human!

Buzz   And beautiful?

Natasha   Not really, no.

Polly   Any chance of a bloody rescue!

Jake   Arm yourselves!

They rush around finding dustbin lids and other detritus to use as shields and weapons, etc.

Jake *finds an old umbrella to use as a sword.*

Much noise and activity.

Jake *stands on an old milk crate.*

The others gather round him and cheer.

They continue to cheer at key moments throughout the following speech –

Jake   Today we do battle! Battle with a terrible Dragon. A ferocious Dragon. A Dragon with jaws like a shark. A Dragon with scales sharp as razors. A Dragon who glitters bright enough to blind! But a Dragon we must fight! And it's a fight we will win! We'll win because we'll fight it together. Individually – we don't stand a chance. But together – oh, look at us! We are invincible! Are we together?

All   Yes!

Jake   (*louder*) Are we united?

All   (*louder*) Yes!

Jake   Then the Dragon is doomed. This Dragon called … Sparkleshark!

All   (*chanting*) Sparkleshark! Sparkleshark! Sparkleshark! Sparkleshark!

Everything explodes into action.

The chanting is loud and vigorous.

Various bits of detritus are used as drums.

Jake, **Natasha**, **Carol**, **Russell**, **Buzz**, **Speed** and **Shane** *pursue the fleeing* **Polly** *and* **Finn** *around the roof.*

Polly *is screaming.*

Finn *is roaring.*

The chanting and general clamour get louder and louder.

Everyone, although taking their various roles very seriously, is thoroughly enjoying themselves.

Buzz, **Speed** *and* **Carol** *help each other over various obstacles etc.*

Likewise, **Shane** *helps* **Natasha**, *and* **Russell** *helps* **Jake**.

Finally, **Finn** *is surrounded.*

He lashes out with his clawed hands.

Polly *watches from one side.*

Finn   RAAAAAGGGHHHHH!!!

Buzz   Get him!

Speed   Kill him!

Carol   Save the Princess!

Slight pause.

Tentatively, **Russell** *approaches* **Finn.**

Jake   No, Prince! This is my job! I'm the one who started it all. I must be the one to end.

Russell   But I'm stronger than you!

Finn   RAAAAAGGGHHHHH!!!

Russell   (*at* **Jake**) You're right! *You* do it!

Jake – *his umbrella raised – approaches* **Finn.**

Finn *is roaring and clawing at him.*

Polly *is screaming.*

The others are avidly cheering **Jake** *on.*

Suddenly, **Finn** *lashes out at* **Jake.**

Jake *cries out and falls to the floor.*

Russell *rushes forward and pulls* **Jake** *away from* **Finn.**

Jake   Wh … what are you doing?

Russell   The Dragon's broken your arm. You can't carry on. Let me take your sword. Please.

Jake *gives* **Russell** *the umbrella.*

Jake   Thank you, Prince.

Carol   Save the Princess!

Buzz   Do it, Prince!

Speed   Do it!

Natasha   Kill the Dragon.

All   (*chanting*) Kill! Kill! Kill! Kill! Kill!

Russell *approaches* **Finn**.

They circle each other for a while.

Everyone cheers, claps, stamps their feet, chants, etc.

Finn *is clawing at* **Russell**.

Russell *is swinging the umbrella.*

They do this in slow motion, exaggerating sound and gesture.

In the course of the ensuing fight, **Russell**'s *umbrella touches* **Finn**'s *arm.*

Finn *lets out a roar.*

Then **Finn** *touches* **Russell**'s *chest.*

Russell *lets out a roar.*

The crowd continues cheering etc.

Finally, **Finn** *is beaten to the ground.*

Russell *raises his umbrella.*

All   KILL! KILL! KILL! KILL! KILL!

Russell   DIE, SPARKLESHARK! DIE!

Then just as **Russell** *is about to strike* –

Polly   STOP!

Polly *rushes to* **Finn** *and cradles his head in her lap.*

Everyone is still and silent.

Polly   This is a *good* Dragon! A *kind* Dragon! Yes, I know it kidnapped me. But look what I did. I destroyed what was in its egg! The egg more beautiful than a million yellow flowers.

Slight pause.

And while I've been on this mountain the Dragon has looked after me. Kept me warm at night. Given me food. And I've learned to understand what it's saying.

Finn   (*softly*) Raaagghhhaaa.

Polly   Yes, my kind Dragon. I'll tell them – Everyone is afraid of him because of what he looks like.

Finn   (*softly*) Raaaghhhaaa.

Polly   At night, the Dragon spreads its magnificent wings and there's no one there to marvel how they sparkle by moonlight.

Finn *starts to weep.*

Slight pause.

Natasha   The Dragon's crying.

Carol   Poor Dragon.

Buzz   Don't cry.

Speed   Don't.

Shane   What can we do to stop him crying?

Slight pause.

Polly   You must lay your hand on the Dragon and say … Oh, tell the Dragon you're his friend.

Slight pause.

Slowly, **Natasha** *approaches* **Finn**.

She kneels beside him.

Lays her hand on him.

Natasha   I'm your friend, Sparkleshark.

Slight pause.

Carol *approaches* **Finn**.

She kneels beside him.

Lays her hand on him.

Carol   I'm your friend, Sparkleshark.

Slight pause.

Buzz *approaches* **Finn**.

He kneels beside him.

Lays his hand on him.

Buzz   I'm your friend, Sparkleshark.

Slight pause.

Speed *approaches* **Finn**.

He kneels beside him.

Lays his hand on him.

Speed   I'm your friend, Sparkleshark.

Slight pause.

Shane *approaches* **Finn**.

He kneels beside him.

Lays his hand on him.

Shane   I'm your friend, Sparkleshark.

Slight pause.

Russell *approaches* **Finn**.

He kneels beside him.

Lays his hand on him.

Russell   I'm your friend, Sparkleshark.

Slight pause.

Jake *approaches* **Finn**.

He kneels beside him.

Lays his hand on him.

Jake   I'm your friend, Sparkleshark.

Slight pause.

Finn   Raaahhh.

Polly   Sparkleshark is your friend too.

Pause.

Jake *stands.*

Jake   And, from that moment on, the land lived in perfect peace. The Prince and Princess lived happily in their Castle. The Wizard and the Witch created planets together. The one-time horses, Thunder and Lightning, became best friends with the one-time frog and nightingale. I – the King – was forgiven. And, at night, if children saw a strange light in the sky, their parents would say, 'Don't worry, my love. That's just moonlight on the Dragon's wings.'

Long, silent pause.

Polly *begins to applaud* **Jake**.

Then **Russell** *begins to applaud.*

Then all the others join in.

They all cheer and congratulate him.

Jake   But it wasn't just me! It was *all* of us! Together! The story belongs to us all!

Russell   Let's do another one! Jake! Another story! Now!

Jake   I can't! Not now! I've got to get home for tea.

Everyone nods and murmurs assent.

Russell   But … we can't just stop there!

Shane   We should meet again.

All   Yeah.

Russell   Next week!

All   Yeah!

Buzz   Same time!

Speed   Same place!

All   Yeah!

Natasha   And we'll tell another story!

Russell   All of us together!

All   Yeah!

Russell   We should call ourselves something!

Buzz   … The Storytelling Group!

All   Nah.

Speed   The S.A.S. – The Secret Association of Storytellers.

All   Nah!

Finn   … Sparkleshark!

Polly   Yes, Finn! That's it! We'll call ourselves 'Sparkleshark'!

All   Yeah! Sparkleshark!

Russell   And we'll have a salute! Our secret sign when we meet each other – the Dragon's claw.

Claws his fist as **Finn** *had done.*

Jake   (*punching air with salute*) Sparkleshark!

All   (*punching air with salute*) Sparkleshark!

Slight pause.

They start making their way up the metal staircase to the raised platform.

Jake *collects his notebook etc. together.*

He is the last to climb.

Russell *helps* **Jake** *onto the raised platform.*

*They all smile at each other and look at the roof around them.
Then –*

*Suddenly and simultaneously, they punch the air with the clawed
salute and –*

All   (*triumphantly*) SPARKLESHARK!

Blackout.

Moonfleece

*There is no greater agony than
an untold story inside you.*

Maya Angelou

Moonfleece was commissioned by the Royal National Theatre, London, as part of the National Connections Festival 2004. It received its professional premiere at The Rich Mix, London on 3 March 2010 with the following cast and creative team:

Link	Reece Noi
Gavin	Ashley George
Tommy	Bradley Taylor
Curtis	Sean Verey
Alex	Krupa Pattani
Jez	David Ames
Sarah	Emily Plumtree
Nina	Sian Robin-Grace
Zak	Beru Tessema
Wayne	Reeda Harris
Stacey	Alicia Davies

Director	David Mercatali
Set and Lighting	William Reynolds
Costume	Ellan Parry
Sound	Ed Borgnis

Characters

Link
Gavin
Tommy
Curtis
Alex
Jez
Sarah
Nina
Zak
Wayne
Stacey

A derelict flat on the top floor of a tower block in East London. The peeling wallpaper and decrepit furniture (small side-table, armchair) indicate the place has not been 'officially' lived in for quite a while. There are, however, signs of more recent 'unofficial' occupation: cans of lager, remains of fast food, a radio, a book, sleeping bag etc.

The boards covering the windows have been removed to reveal cracked, broken or missing glass (and afternoon sunlight). A few doors: to kitchen, balcony and the front door (broken off at hinges). A hallway in the flat leads, presumably, to bedrooms and bathroom.

A political banner can be seen. It has a family photo on it: smiling middle-aged couple, two sons (late teens, early twenties) and a twenty-year old woman (who, judging from the held hands and engagement rings, is the eldest son's fiancée). They are all neatly dressed and (very, very) smiling. Also, a pile of fliers, a megaphone, a box of badges (everything emblazoned with the cross of St George and 'VOTE AVALON').

The sound of distant barking can be heard. This is loud to begin with but rapidly fades away.

Link *stands in the middle of the flat. He is fifteen years old and wearing scruffy jeans and trainers.*

Link   Who d'you think you are? Eh? You can't just march in here and do what you fucking like. You don't own the bloody place.

Tommy *has come in from kitchen. He is eighteen years old and wearing a neat, dove-grey suit. His hair, like the rest of him, is slick and tidy. He is muscular and tall for his age, a graceful giant at home with tea cups and sledgehammers. He looks round room as –*

Link   You've scared the dogs! Hear them? They can go on for hours like that, you know – Don't touch that!

Tommy *has picked up book.*

He flicks through it.

Gavin *enters from hallway. He is seventeen years old and, like Tommy, wearing a dove-grey suit. Unlike* **Tommy**, *however, the effect is totally incongruous. Short, stocky and generally ungainly, he's like a Rottweiler in a tutu.*

Link   I don't live here alone, you know. Oh, no. My mate lives here too. If he comes back and catches you – Oh, you'll be in trouble. *Big* trouble. I can go and get him. Easy. I know where he is. He's down by the supermarket. If I screamed from the balcony – I bet he'd hear me.

Tommy *gets mobile phone from his pocket.*

Gavin   My turn to call!

Gets mobile from his pocket.

… What'll I say?

Tommy   Tell him we're in the flat.

Gavin *dials.*

Link   My mate – he's older than me, you know. Oh, yeah. He's strong. Big. Zak looks after me. Zak can do things with his little finger you couldn't do with your … with a grenade launching bazooka.

Gavin   Voice mail.

Tommy   Message.

Gavin   Curtis. Gavin. Place secure. Awaiting further instructions. Over and out.

Link   'Over and out'? Who's he bloody think he is? The S. A. S.?

Gavin   Shut it!

Link   Why should I?

Gavin   Because you value your kneecaps.

Tommy   Gav!

Gavin   It's *him*!

Points at **Link**.

Tommy   (*to* **Link**) Listen. Why don't you make yourself scarce for an hour or so? Here's some money. Get yourself something to eat.

Link   Stuff your money! This is *my* place.

Gavin   Your *squat*!

Link   I've still got rights!

Gavin   You've got nothing!

Tommy   Gavin!

Gavin   You're an illegal immigrant!

Link   I'm not.

Gavin   What's your bloody name, then?

Link   Why should I tell you!?

Gavin   Illegal! I can *smell* it on him.

Link   Piss off!

Gavin   What's your bloody name?

Link   Rumple – bloody – Stiltskin.

Gavin   Not English!

Tommy   He's playing with you, for chrissakes.

Gavin   Eh?

Tommy   It's from a kid's story!

Gavin   You bastard –

Makes a dash for **Link**.

Link *darts out of the way.*

Tommy   Gavin! ... Gav!

Holds **Gavin** *back.*

Link　My mate'll kill you – you hurt me!

Tommy　(*at* **Link**) No one's gonna hurt you.

Gavin　No?

Tommy　No! Stop it! … Stop!

Gavin　… He's winding me up, Tommy.

Tommy　You're winding yourself up! Okay? Now cool it … Cool it!

Gavin *calms down.*

Tommy *lets go of him.*

Tommy　Okay. Now … Let's all take a deep breath and start again, shall we.

Slight pause.

(*at* **Link**) My name is Tommy. This is Gavin. What's yours?

Link *doesn't answer.*

Tommy　Okay. Look … we're sorry we knocked down your door. That was very wrong of us. Wasn't it, Gav?

Silence.

Okay. We knocked it down because we were unaware anyone was living here.

Link　You could've bloody knocked.

Gavin　It's a derelict bloody tower block, you foreign bastard.

Tommy　Alright! I accept – *we* accept – we should've knocked. We're sorry. We weren't thinking. Were we, Gavin?

Gavin *doesn't answer.*

Tommy　Okay. Me and Gavin – we've been very busy lately, you see, and sometimes … well, sometimes we get a bit carried away … we didn't mean any harm … Honestly …

Link *is looking at banners etc.*

Gavin   Don't touch those.

Tommy   He can bloody touch them for chrissakes! – We're campaigning. There's an election next week.

Link   I know that. Not stupid.

Gavin   No?

Link   No! ... Tell me, why haven't you put your *real* symbol on this lot?

Gavin   (*at* **Tommy**) What's he mean?

Link   You see, if you'd put your *real* symbol on all this then I would have understood. I mean ... I would have known exactly who I was dealing with. All your huffing and your puffing and your blowing my door down.

Gavin   He's a bloody retard.

Tommy   Gav!

Link   Tattoos! You must have had it tattooed on you somewhere.

Gavin   You're winding me up again.

Tommy   No, he's not – Tattoo?

Link   Yeah. Come on! Show me!

Tommy   I don't understand what you – ?

Link   Your swastikas!

Gavin   It's prejudiced comments like that get your head kicked in!

Tommy   Gav!

Gavin   He's ignorant.

Tommy   Well, we're not gonna educate him by shouting.

Link   I don't *need* educating about you lot.

Tommy   We are an official political party.

Gavin   We take old people on day trips to Southend.

Link   *White* old people!

Gavin   Pakis don't like the seaside.

Tommy   Gav! Jesus! Remember what Mr Avalon says. 'Don't heckle a heckler. Educate through –' Gav? What does Mr Avalon say? Educate through …?

Gavin   … Reasonable debate.

Link   Oh! You can *reasonably* debate, can you?

Gavin   Yes!

Link   This I *must* see! Go on. Debate. Reasonably.

Slight pause.

Tommy   Go on, Gav.

Link   Go on, Gav.

Gavin   … Good evening, ladies and gentlemen.

Link   It's afternoon.

Tommy   Think before you speak, Gav.

Link   Ooo, getting tricky, eh, Gav?

Gavin   … Good afternoon, ladies and gentleman – Just gentlemen! I want to thank you all for coming out on such a chilly night. Warm day –

Points at **Link**.

Gavin   (*at* **Tommy**) He's laughing at me!

Tommy   Perhaps you should skip the introduction and go to the next bit … 'I'd like to introduce you to –'

Gavin   I know, I know!

Indicates photo on banner.

I'd like to introduce you to a family. They've been an important family in my life and hopefully they'll become an important family in yours. This is Mr Avalon. You might have seen him around. He's lived in East London all his life. His Dad lived here before him. Mr Avalon can trace his family roots back to William the Conqueror.

Link   Who was French.

Gavin   Says who?

Tommy   Just … just carry on.

Gavin   This is Mrs Avalon. She's East London born and bred too. She's the perfect mum and wife is Mrs Avalon. No one cooks roast beef like her. This is their eldest son. His name's Wayne. And this is Wayne's fiancée, the beautiful Stacey. They got engaged when they were sixteen. Childhood sweethearts. Next year – on Wayne's twenty-second birthday – they're gonna get married. It will be the biggest bash East London's seen in years. Who knows? If you're a friend of the family – like me – you might get an invitation too.

Link   Bet it's gonna be a really white wedding, eh?

Tommy   Why don't you give him a chance?

Gavin   This is Curtis! Curtis is the youngest son! He's eighteen. He's left school now and is working in his Dad's double-glazing business down Mile End Road. Curtis is a bit of a thinker. He's got a shelf full of books in his room –

Link *yawns and walks away.*

Gavin   Oi!

Grabs megaphone and yells through it –

We don't believe in honour killings here.

Tommy   That's right!

Gavin   We don't believe in banning music or dancing here. We don't believe in stoning people to death here.

Tommy   What *do* we believe in?

Gavin   We believe in the history and tradition of this great nation. Our aim is to give this nation back its self-respect. To do that we've got to rediscover the spirit and values that made us rule the waves.

Tommy   Go for it, mate!

Gavin   The family!

Tommy   Yes!

Gavin   Moral values.

Tommy   Christian values.

Gavin   For this is a Christian country.

Tommy   Always has been.

Gavin   Royalty! Tradition!

Tommy   Work ethic!

Gavin   Respect for the law!

Tommy   Neighbour helping neighbour.

Gavin   A clean doorstep!

Tommy   The Blitz spirit reborn!

Gavin   This is the future I see.

Tommy   Who can give us this future?

Gavin and **Tommy**   (*chanting*) Avalon ... Avalon ... Avalon ...

Distant dogs, disturbed by the noise once again, start barking as –

Curtis *arrives in doorway, holding a torch. He is eighteen years old and wearing a dove-grey suit that fits him to perfection. He is fair haired, glossily good looking, as slick and smooth as a shark in baby oil. He watches as –*

Gavin and **Tommy**   (*chanting*) Avalon ... Avalon –

Gavin *and* **Tommy** *see* **Curtis**.

Tommy   Oh … Hello, Curtis.

Gavin   Hello, Curtis.

Curtis   Your racket set the dogs off.

Tommy   Sorry, mate. We … er … we got a little carried away.

The noise of the dogs starts to fade.

Gavin   I've been educating someone, Curtis.

Indicates **Link**.

Gavin   I've been giving him the full Gav treatment.

Link   It worked! I'm a convert! – Sieg heil, Curtis!

Gives Nazi salute.

Gavin   Oi! Respect! – And keep your distance!

Stands between **Curtis** *and* **Link**.

Curtis   (*indicating* **Link**) Tommy?

Tommy   Says he lives here. Two of them apparently. Other one's out somewhere.

Gavin   Begging probably.

Link   He's a street entertainer.

Gavin   Exactly! – You get my message Curt? I left a message with an update. Did you get it?

Curtis   No.

Tommy   I've informed this individual we'll only be requiring the premises for a short period but he still refuses to vacate.

Curtis   I'm sure he'll go if you ask him nicely – Won't you?

Link   Bollocks!

Gavin   Oi! Don't forget who you're talking to.

Link   I haven't! Bollocks! Know what you lot did? Last place I lived? Went around throwing pigs heads into Mosques. Their idea of fun. You make me sick. All of you. You're nothing but scum! Scum!

Curtis   … I'll deal with you later.

Link   Ooo, you're turning me on!

Gavin   Don't be disgusting!

Link   *Me* disgusting!?

Curtis *starts looking round the flat.*

Link   So … what's your story, eh? You lot? Wanna use this place for a secret H.Q. or something? Print hate mail? Make petrol bombs?

Curtis   Where's the table and stuff, Tom?

Tommy   What table and stuff?

Curtis   The fold up table. The one from the back of the meeting hall. And chairs. They're supposed to be here.

Tommy   First I've heard.

Curtis *stares at* **Gavin**.

Tommy *follows the stare.*

Tommy   Bloody hell, Gav.

Gavin   I put everything in the back of the car.

Curtis   So where's the car?

Gavin   Down by the museum.

Curtis   Well, it's not doing much good there, is it?

Gavin   It's *him*!

Points at **Tommy**.

Tommy   Me?

Gavin We were in the car, Curtis. I was giving it the ol' 'Vote Avalon' business out the window. Going great guns, I was. We had some time to spare. *He* suggested we park the car and walk through Bethnal Green Road market. There I was! 'Vote Avalon'. Flyers! Badges. We got all the way down to the supermarket. We stood outside for a while. Twenty people told me we had their vote in all, Curtis. Twenty! Not bad, eh?

Curtis Cut to the chase!

Gavin (*pointing at* **Tommy**) *He* said it wasn't worth going back for the car.

Tommy I didn't know there was stuff in the boot we needed, did I!

Gavin You didn't bloody ask!

Tommy Gimme strength!

Curtis Hang on! Don't tell me you walked up those stairs without a torch.

Gavin *gets lighter from pocket and lights it.*

Gavin I lit the way with this, Curt!

Curtis You said you'd quit smoking.

Gavin … I'm trying!

Curtis No ciggies. No drink. No nothing. We've got to be squeaky clean. You know that.

Gavin Sorry.

Tommy Want me to go back for them?

Curtis Eh? What?

Tommy The chairs and table.

Curtis There's no time now. It's gonna kick off any minute.

Link What's gonna 'kick off'?

Gavin Your head if you don't piss off!

Curtis   Gavin! Jesus! … A word, mate – Come here.

Slight pause.

Gavin *goes over to* **Curtis**.

Curtis   If you use any more language like that I will be forced to tell Dad and –

Gavin   But, Curt –

Curtis   No, no, listen, mate, listen. You've been warned before.

Gavin   … I know.

Curtis   *What* were you warned? Tell me.

Gavin   No … no bad language.

Curtis   No bad language. And no threatening language.

Gavin   I've been trying. I really have.

Curtis   Well, try a bit harder. Wayne won't come to your rescue every time.

Gavin   The party's everything to me.

Curtis   I know that, mate. Now, put your thinking cap on and let's solve the table and chairs situation. Can you do that for me?

Gavin   Sure thing, Curt.

Looks at **Tommy**, *then indicates* **Link**.

Curtis   Give him some money.

Link   I don't need your money. This is *my* place!

Curtis   No. It's not.

Gavin   What about this?

Points at small side-table.

Curtis   It's … not quite big enough, mate. We all need to sit around it.

Gavin   Armchair?

Curtis   No.

Gavin   Two people can sit on the arms and –

Curtis   No! We need a proper table with proper chairs like I told you to bloody – Jesus! Tommy?

Tommy   We'll check the other flats. Might strike lucky. How many chairs?

Curtis   Three.

Tommy   No worries – Oi! Mr Memory!

Tommy *and* **Gavin** *leave.*

Link *is looking at the Avalon family photo on the banner.*

Link   So … what's it like having your family photo used as a piece of political propaganda?

Curtis   … It's fine.

Link   This your garden?

Curtis   Eh?

Link   Where the photo was taken.

Curtis   Yes.

Link   The roses look … a bit odd.

Curtis   They were put in afterwards.

Link   What?

Curtis   Photoshop. The roses were sort of … pasted on or something. I dunno. That's Wayne's department.

Link   Your brother?

Curtis   My *step* brother.

Sound of distant door being kicked in.

Dogs start barking.

Link   Your mates've turned door kicking into an art form.

Curtis   Tommy's a trained athlete.

Link   Crowbars're easier. You just get it under the lock and –
crack! Open says-a-me.

Curtis   The crowbar and other useful items are in the car. As you
heard.

Link   Your mates – they're not the sharpest knives in the
dishwater, are they.

Curtis   Shut up! There's nothing wrong with Tommy!

Has been dialling on his mobile phone and now –

Hi . I'm in the flat … Yeah, yeah, odd. Very odd … Thought you
might be here by now … You finished at four on Saturdays, you
said … Oh, right … Look, forget buses, Sarah. Call a mini cab.
I'll pay … Sarah, we can't run late. It's gonna get dark and there's
no lighting here, you know … Okay, okay … Call up when you
arrive and I'll send Tommy down with the cab money … Good …
And Sarah? Thanks.

Hangs up.

Link   So … who's Sarah?

Sound of dogs has faded now.

Curtis *looks round flat.*

Link   Girlfriend?

No answer.

Link   You *want* her as a girlfriend?

No answer.

Link   *Ex*-girlfriend!

Curtis   Shut it!

Another door kicked in.

Dogs bark.

Link   So … why's *ex*-girlfriend Sarah coming here?

Curtis   What's it to you?

Link   I have a natural curiosity in every Fascist who invades my home!

Curtis   It's *my* home!

Link   Of course. *Everything* belongs to you lot, doesn't it.

Curtis   No. Not everything. But *this* flat – You see that armchair? There was another one like that. Here. A sofa – here! There? Telly! There was a big mirror up here. Photos on the mantelpiece. Ornaments. A snow globe. And in the bedroom at the end of the corridor – In the end room? Are there … paintings on the wall?

Link   Yeah. Fairytale stuff.

Curtis   God. Still there.

Rushes for bedroom, then hesitates.

Link   Go on! What's stopping you?

Curtis   … Nothing.

Link   Did *you* paint them?

Curtis   No. My brother did.

Link   My mate thinks they're amazing. He loves fairytales. We've got a book with them in. See? We look at one a night. He's teaching me to read. He's a great teacher. When he tells a story … everything else – all my problems – they all just float away. It's like you're *in* the story. You know?

Curtis   … Yeah.

Link   Zak tells stories on the street. That's my mate. Zak. I help him sometimes. I'm the official Storyteller Apprentice. I say, 'Ladies and gentleman! Roll up, roll up. Spare us a few minutes of your time and enter a world of enchantment and wonder. We bring you stories! Fantasy. Thriller. Thriller-fantasy. Comedy-weepie-fantasy! Zak here will spin a tale of surprise and magic before your very eyes. Nothing is prepared. Just call out three things and Zak will spin a web of a story to take your breath away.'

Curtis   And does he?

Link   Yeah. Always. Most people clear off. Some stay to hear the whole thing, though. I go round and collect money.

Slight pause.

Tell you one thing. You're brother's better at painting on walls than all this photo whatsit?

Curtis   Eh – ?

Link   These pasted on roses.

Curtis   Oh, that's not *him*, for chrissakes. That's Wayne. I told you. My *step* brother.

Link   So … who did the paintings in the bedroom?

Curtis   Jason. My *real* brother.

Link   So … who's your step parent? Mum or dad?

Curtis   … No more questions.

Link   Why not? I'm not going anywhere. I'm naturally inquisitive. Zak says I'm the chattiest chatterbox he's ever met. Gets me in trouble sometimes.

Curtis   It's getting you in trouble now.

Link   I just wanna know who your step parent is. What's the big deal? I bet it's your mum.

Curtis   No.

Link   Aha! It's your dad!

Another door.

More dogs.

Link   So … what's up with Jason, then?

Curtis   What?

Link   No real brother Jason with real mummy in propaganda family photo.

Curtis   You've got three seconds to disappear.

Link   Or what?

Curtis   One!

Link   Real brother Jason disagree with the step-family politics, eh?

Curtis   Two.

Link *doesn't move.*

Slight pause.

Link   Two and a half?

Curtis   What's wrong with you?

Link   What's wrong with *me*?

Curtis   All I'm asking you to do is give me some … some time here …

Link   This is *my* place!

Curtis   Jesus Christ, haven't you heard *anything* I've said, you bloody stupid – ? Listen! My Gran was one of the first people to move into this tower block. My Mum – she was born in this flat. She had her wedding reception in this flat. My Mum and Dad lived in this flat. My first Dad. My *real* Dad. When Gran died the funeral procession left from this flat. The big bedroom down the hall? That's where Jason was born. Me too. The four of us lived here and we were bloody happy. Mum, Dad, Jason and me. Everyone respected Mum and Dad. They came to them for advice and stuff. If anyone had a complaint against a neighbour they didn't go to the council or anything. They went to Mum. They went to Dad. *They* sorted it out. Always. When Dad died – I tell you, the whole bloody block stood outside when the hearse drove passed. And the flowers! The car park was covered. You could smell them right down to the supermarket. Local papers took photographs. We had drinks and

sandwiches in here afterwards. Neighbours queued up for hours –
hours! – to pay their respects. You see this armchair? Mum sat here
and cried so much the cushions were wet for weeks. Months. Dad's
death ripped her to bloody pieces. You ever seen that happen to
someone you love? Eh? It's shit! I'd rather kill myself than see that
again! My brother – Jason, my *real* brother – he had to look after
me. He was seven years older. He washed my clothes and got me to
school and … and cooked my dinner and … – Don't you *dare* refer
to this flat as yours! Hear me? Don't *dare*! It'll *never* be yours! It'll
never be anyone's except mine. Even when they dynamite the place
– and it's nothing but rubble – the rubble that makes up this flat
will have my name running through it!

Alex   (*off, calling*) Sarah?

Link   Who's that?

Alex   Sarah?

Curtis   Jesus …

Alex *strides in, holding torch. She is eighteen years old and
wearing combat trousers, T-shirt and denim jacket. Her hair is
short and tousled. Confident and swaggering, she seems to be
constantly on the precipice of an argument and relishing the
prospect of jumping in head first.*

Alex   (*at* **Curtis**) Jesus, what's this? Suited and booted like a
normal person? That's not fooling anyone, Curtis. Not when you
still reek of the Third Reich.

Curtis   What you doing here?

Alex   Sarah not turned up yet?

Curtis   Alex!?

Alex   I'm here for Sarah!

Curtis   Did she *ask* you to come?

Alex   I'm surprising her.

Curtis   Why're you always sticking your big bloody nose in?

Alex   Let's think. Perhaps it like … Yeah! Like when I'm watching Sleeping Beauty. The bit where the Princess is using the spinning wheel. You know? The wicked whatever has put poison on the prick of the needle. Every time I watch that scene I can't help sticking my big bloody nose in and calling out, 'Don't go near the poisoned prick!'

Link *laughs.*

Alex   Oh, hello, mate – Hang on! Don't tell me! You live here, right?

Link   They kicked my door in.

Alex   (*at* **Curtis**) Pig!

Hold hands out to **Link***.*

Alex   Alex.

Link   Link.

Alex   Oh?

Link   When I was a kid I kept running away. So … the missing –

Alex   The missing Link! I like it.

Link   Yeah, me too.

Alex   You and me'll stick together, Link. We'll be the underground freedom fighters against the Imperial Storm Troopers.

Curtis   What did Sarah tell you?

Alex   About?

Curtis   This!

Alex   Everything.

Curtis   Jesus! She promised she wouldn't tell anyone.

Alex   I am not *anyone*, pal.

Link   What they doing here, Alex?

Curtis   Not a word.

Alex   Hitler Youth here has seen a ghost.

Link   A ghost!

Gavin *and* **Tommy** *can be heard struggling in with table.*

Alex   Oh, no. Don't tell me. Not all three ugly sisters in one room. This is too good to be true.

Gavin *and* **Tommy** *appear with table.*

Alex   Hello, ladies.

Gavin   What's she doing here?

Curtis   Nothing to do with me.

Tommy   You're not welcome, Alex.

Alex   From you, that's a compliment.

Link   What ghost you been seeing?

Curtis   Shut it!

Alex   Pig!

Gavin *and* **Tommy** *are having trouble with the table.*

Tommy   Careful!

Gavin   It's you!

Jez   (*calling, off*) Al-lex?

Curtis   Jesus! Who's that?

Alex   Jez! – You alright, babes?

Jez   Where are you, babes?

Alex   Walk to the end of the corridor.

Jez   I'm lost, babes!

Alex   Hang on, babes.

Tries to get past **Gavin** *and* **Tommy**.

Curtis   Who the hell's this Jez?

Alex   You bringing that table in, boys, or is this some sexual fetish of yours?

Gavin   Don't be disgusting!

Curtis   Alex! Who's this Jez?

Alex   A mate!

Goes to grab table.

Gavin   Hands off our table!

Alex   *Your* table!?

Link   They own *everything*!

Curtis   This ain't some bloody free for all, you know. I don't want the whole world and his bloody cousin to – Jesus!

Starts dialling on mobile.

Alex   Phoning Sarah? Go ahead! What d'you think she's gonna say? 'Ooo, tell that pesky Alex to clear off, Curt-baby?' You arrogant pig! I'm surprised she's agreed to come here at all after what you did.

Tommy   What did *he* bloody do?

Alex   You can't be serious?

Curtis   *Sarah* stopped talking to *me*!

Tommy   That's right!

Curtis   No reason!

Alex   No *reason*? You want the full essay or just the bullet points? You lied! You're full of hate! You preach hate! Your views stink! You're a pig! You'll breed pigs! Want me to carry on?

Tommy   Shut up.

Alex   You took that precious thing – the most precious thing in the whole world – and you shat on it from a great height. 'Oh, you should see us when we're alone, Alex. He's so affectionate. I look into his big eyes and – ' Big eyes? The wolf had big eyes! And teeth! The teeth you lied through, you heartless piece of –

Tommy   Leave him alone.

Alex   What was it you said to her? 'Oh, I'm not really part of all this Avalon stuff, Sarah. I'm not political. I just go along with it because I don't wanna upset Mum.' Then what happens? A little secretive Easter rally in the middle of Epping Forest. A family day out with smiley grannies and toddlers chanting, 'England for the white!' We hid behind the trees. I watched her when she heard you speak. Her world fell apart.

Curtis   She would never've known about it if it weren't for you.

Tommy   That's right.

Alex   I had a *duty* to tell her.

Curtis   A *duty*!?

Alex   Yes! As her friend. To show her what you really are.

Tommy   What you did broke Sarah's heart.

Curtis   *I'd* never treat a friend like that.

Tommy   Nor me.

Alex   I can't … I can't believe what I'm bloody hearing – Jesus! Now, you listen to me, you pair of delusional scumbags. It wasn't *me* who broke her to pieces! It was me who picked up the pieces. It was me who held her when she cried. She was on medication for months. You know that? Course you don't! Not even a bloody phone call.

Link   You could've bloody phoned.

Curtis   I *did* phone.

Tommy   Sarah wouldn't speak to him.

Alex   Not even a card when she jumped in the canal and tried to … Oh, shit! Shit!

Curtis   '*Jumped*?' … Alex?

Alex   … Forget it.

Curtis   I heard … I was *told* she slipped and fell into the canal. An *accident* … Tom?

Tommy   That's what I was told.

Gavin   Me too.

Alex   It's what *everyone* was told! Okay? It's what her family wanted. Sarah got a little drunk one night and slipped into the canal. Her friends – me included – had to fish her out. Everyone was giggling. All a bit of a laugh. But it wasn't a bloody laugh. Far from it. Now you know.

Jez   (*calling, off*) Alex?

Alex   Yes!

Alex strides over to table and effortlessly lifts it high.

She plonks it down and leaves.

Slight pause.

Tommy   … Okay. Let's get the table in place, shall we?

Curtis   Tom … Sarah – she tried to …

Tommy   We can't think of that now, mate.

Curtis   You *swear* you didn't know.

Tommy   I'd *never* lie to you, mate. You *know* that.

Curtis   Yeah, mate. I know.

Gavin   Oi! Lovebirds! Where's the table going?

Tommy   Well, let's see … .

Picks up table.

(*at* **Link**) Get out the way.

Link *moves*.

Tommy   About here, Curt?

Puts table down.

Curt?

Curtis   What? Oh, yeah, fine.

Curtis*'s mobile rings.*

He checks it.

Curtis   … Tom?

Tommy   Sarah?

Curtis *nods.*

The mobile continues ringing.

Tommy   You gonna answer it, mate?

Slight pause.

Curtis *hands mobile out to* **Tommy***.*

Tommy *takes mobile and answers it.*

Tommy   (*into mobile*) Hi, Sarah, it's Tom … Okay, I'll be right down.

Gives phone back to **Curtis***.*

Tommy   Everything's alright, mate. Don't worry.

Curtis *doesn't respond.*

Tommy   Come here. Relax.

Rubs **Curtis***'s shoulders.*

Curtis   There's no time for that, mate.

Tommy   No one wins a fight when they're tense.

Gavin   *I'm* tense.

Tommy   That's how you're *meant* to bloody be!

Continues to rub **Curtis***'s shoulders.*

Tommy   You're all knots and tangles … There … Better?

Curtis   Thanks, Tom.

Tommy   (*at* **Gavin**) Come on, Mr Tense!

Tommy *strides out followed by* **Gavin**.

Slight pause.

Link   So … was it someone you knew?

Curtis   Eh? Who?

Link   The ghost.

Curtis   Yeah, yeah. Someone I knew.

Link   Was it your *real* dad?

Curtis   No.

Link   Then who?

Curtis   I … I'd rather not talk about it. Please.

Link   I saw a ghost once. The last foster place I was in. A kid from years ago. Said he'd been chopped up and buried in the cellar. Foster couple looked so kind and cosy. Don't think it was them did the chopping. Mind you, you never can tell. The bloke collected beer mats so something weren't right. I'd like to collect sea shells but I've got nowhere to keep them. Do you collect anything?

Curtis   Do I – ? Look! Don't take this the wrong way but I'm not really in the mood to shoot the breeze about – oh, Christ! The taxi money! Tommy! Wait! Tom!

Rushes out as **Alex** *and* **Jez** *come in.*

They collide.

Alex   Don't let us get in your way, will you! Pig!

Curtis *has gone, calling after* **Tommy**.

Jez *is seventeen years old. His clothes are stylish and casual. Like Alex, there is something brave and fearless about him. He is carrying a small bag, a torch and voice recorder.*

Link   Sarah's downstairs.

Alex   She's here, Jez!

Rushes to balcony.

Jez   Look at this place! Am I Aladdin in the cave or what? – Oh! Link, I presume.

Link   Us three against the Imperial Storm Troopers, eh?

Jez   You bet, babes.

Talks into voice recorder.

I am talking to Link who is the current occupant of 127, Sunrise Heights – now commonly known as Wild Dog Heights – the top floor flat where Curtis Avalon was born. Tell me, Link, how long have you been here?

Link   Er … almost a week.

Jez   And what is your first impression of Curtis?

Link   He's a pig.

Jez   Agreed. But do you think he's a *sexy* pig?

Link   What?

Alex *has come back in looking a little shell-shocked.*

Alex   Oh, Jez.

Jez   Babes? What's up?

Alex   She's wearing the new dress.

Jez   Not the one *you* bought her?

Alex   It was an anniversary present. Two years of wonderful friendship. And now she wears it to come here and … and meet …

Link   Perhaps it was the only clean dress she had.

Jez   Exactly. Thank you, Link – Babes! You gonna let the Fascists see you upset? Eh? … Eh?

Alex   Who's upset? Me? Ha!

Jez   That's my babes.

Link   What's all this for?

Indicates voice recorder.

Jez   What – ? Oh, I'm doing a – how shall I say – a study of Curtis.

Link   Why?

Jez   I want to get into his mind.

Alex   Into his pants more like.

Jez   My, someone ate a big bowl of wisecracks for breakfast.

Link   How can you fancy that Fascist?

Jez   'I Was A Teenage Fascist Fancier.' How's that for a title?

Alex   Jez has a theory about Curtis.

Link   What theory?

Jez   Why he became a Fascist. And it's not a theory! It's fact!

Link   What is it?

Jez   Guilt!

Link   How come?

Jez   The state his Mum got in after his Dad – his *real* dad – was killed.

Link   Curtis's real Dad was … *killed*!?

Alex   Murdered.

Link   What happened?

Alex   Oh, you don't want to hear all the –

Jez   Gruesome details? Course he does.

Link   Course I do.

Alex   Well, *you* tell him, then.

Jez   No. Curtis told Sarah and Sarah told *you*. So *you're* nearest to the source as they say in journalist circles. Besides, I haven't heard you tell it since I got this.

Indicates voice recorder.

(*into voice recorder*) The story of the fateful night of Curtis's *real* dad's death as told by Alex Pattani while sitting in the very flat where the deceased man lived and died. Wow! – Alex?

Alex   Curtis's Dad went down to the supermarket and –

Jez   Set the scene. Come on, babes. Snow.

Slight pause.

Alex   It was snowing. Winter.

Jez   December.

Alex   Curtis wasn't very well.

Jez   Nor was his brother.

Link   Jason.

Jez   Who told you about Jason?

Link   Curtis.

Jez   Lordy, he must really like you. What's your secret?

Link   I just ask a lot of questions.

Alex   Curtis and Jason had been out playing in the snow.

Jez   Victoria Park. The lake was frozen.

Alex   The brothers caught a chill or something. Although, from what Sarah says, Curtis was a sickly child generally.

Jez   Hard to believe when you see him now.

Alex   Oh, perr-leease.

Link   The murder!

Alex   Curtis's mum asked Dad to go down to the chemist and get one of those lemon powder things.

Link   To make a lemon drink?

Alex   Exactly. So Dad goes down to the supermarket and gets the lemon powder and –

Jez   A bit more 'oomph', babes.

Alex   'Oomph'?

Link   Jez is right. You need to create the pictures a bit more. *Feel* it.

Jez   Exactly

Link   If *you* feel it, then *we* will feel it. And we'll follow you anywhere.

Slight pause.

Alex   It's a blizzard! Howling wind! Icicles on every window sill!

Link   The very concrete is shivering!

Jez   Oh, I like that.

Alex   Who's that man making his way across the car park?

Link   It's Curtis's Dad!

Alex   He looks so cold. His fingers are blue with cold.

Link   He's just bought lemon powders for his sick sons.

Jez   He needs to get home as quick as –

Alex   Muggers!

Link   No!

Jez   They jump out of the dark.

Alex   They're hitting and kicking Curtis's Dad.

Link   They want his money.

Alex   Dad won't give it to them. They struggle. Dad falls to the ground. The muggers run off.

Link   Did they get away with anything?

Alex   His wallet.

Jez   And wristwatch.

Alex   But not the lemon powders.

Jez   They've fallen to the snow.

Alex   Dad picks them up.

Jez   He starts to walk home.

Link   Is he hurt?

Alex   He's dripping with blood.

Jez   He leaves a trail behind him.

Link   Like a trail of breadcrumbs.

Jez   Blood red breadcrumbs!

Link   Like rose petals.

Jez   Oh, yesss!

Link   A trail of rose petals in the snow.

Jez   Oh, yesss!

Alex   … You two finished?

Jez and **Link**   Sorry.

Alex   Dad gets back to the tower block. The lifts ain't working. He walks up the stairs.

Jez   All twenty-one floors.

Link   A rose petal of blood on every step.

Jez   Oh, yesss!

Alex   Stop it! … Dad opens the front door to the flat.

Curtis *has stepped into room, unseen by* **Alex**.

Alex   Dad walks down the hall. Dad walks into the room – this room! – and –

Sees **Curtis**.

Slight pause.

Curtis   Don't stop on my account.

Alex   … Curtis's real Dad is covered in blood. Mum screams. Jason screams. Curtis screams. And Curtis's real Dad falls dead. There! Right in front of his whole family.

Curtis   Almost. He died in hospital later that night. He'd been stabbed seven times.

Link   I'm sorry.

Jez   Were you with him when he died?

Curtis   Yes.

Jez   Any his last words?

Curtis   No … Anything else?

Link   Were they caught?

Curtis   The killers? Course not. Black faces into the black night.

Alex   Or white faces into the white snow.

Curtis   Dad knew the difference between black and white.

Sees **Jez** *holding microphone towards him.*

Curtis   Hang on! What's all this?

Link   He's studying you.

Alex   It's for the magazine.

Jez   *R.Y.A.P. Monthly.*

Alex   *Rainbow Youth Against Prejudice.*

Jez   We meet at the library.

Alex   Every Thursday evening.

Jez   You're more than welcome to join.

Curtis   Gimme that!

Grabs for the recorder.

Jez   Fuck off!

Curtis   You've got no right to be here.

Jez   On the contrary, mein fuhrer. I have every right. This tower block is now a public space. Ergo, whatever happens here is, in journalist terms, up for grabs so – to coin a phrase – tough bloody titties.

Has taken a camera from his bag and now takes a photo of **Curtis** *– Flash!*

Curtis   Stop that.

Jez   Public space.

Flash!

Curtis   That's it! The whole thing's cancelled.

Alex   What?

Curtis   You heard!

Dials phone.

Jez *takes a photo – Flash!*

Curtis   I'm warning you!

Jez   He's *so* sexy when he's angry.

Takes another photo.

Curtis *faces wall, his back to front door.*

Curtis   (*into mobile*) Sarah, I'm calling it off … Well, Tommy's told you who's here, I suppose … Yes! But she's brought this Jez pillock.

Alex   Jez pillock?

Jez   Sounds like a detergent.

Curtis   No, Sarah, he's taking photos and stuff.

Jez   'Buy Jezpillock for those stubborn Fascist stains.'

Curtis   This is supposed to be private, Sarah! Me, you, Tommy – No! Go back down stairs. I'm sorry for the trouble. I was stupid to go ahead with something like this in the first place. I must have been mad or something.

Sarah *has appeared, holding mobile to ear. She is seventeen years old and wearing a simple and stylish dress. She's obviously had her hair done and her make-up is slight but very effective. She is carrying a bag.*

Alex *and* **Jez** *watch, expectant.*

Curtis   Sarah? You there? Can you hear me?

Sarah   Yes.

Curtis *freezes.*

Slight pause.

Sarah   Hello, Curtis.

Curtis *keeps his back to her.*

Curtis   … Hello.

Slight pause.

Sarah   You gonna look at me?

Curtis   Yeah. Course I am.

Slowly – oh, so slowly – Curtis turns.

Slight pause.

Sarah   This place … everything looks so small.

Curtis   … Yeah.

Sarah   I remember it being … you know.

Curtis   Yeah.

Jez *takes a photo – Flash!*

Curtis   There! *That's* what I'm talking about!

Sarah   Hello, you two.

Jez   Couldn't let you come here alone, could we?

Alex   Especially in a dress like that.

Sarah   I wore it for work, Al. We had the chief librarian round this afternoon. Official visit. I had to look my best. So … I wore my best.

Alex   And that's the *only* reason?

Sarah   The *only* reason.

Link   I'm Link.

Sarah   Hello.

Nina   (*off, calling*) Sarah! Coo-eee! Sar-rah?

Sarah   Nina! – You okay, Neen?

Gavin *and* **Tommy** *appear, carrying Nina in a wheelchair. She is twenty years old and wearing a bright green dress and lots of jewellery (mostly green and blue glass). Her hair has been tinted to suit her generally aqua-marine appearance.*

Nina   Careful! Stop jolting me! Talk about a life on the ocean waves.

Tommy   Stop rocking her, Gav!

Gavin   It's you!

Alex   Get out the way.

Nudges **Gavin** *aside.*

Nina   Hello, my dear.

Alex   Hello, gorgeous.

Nina   They give me the giant from the beanstalk on this side and ... one of the seven dwarfs on the other.

Link   Dopey.

Link, **Alex**, **Jez** *and* **Nina** *laugh.*

Gavin   Shut up! – (*at* **Curtis** *and* **Tommy**) Why don't you stick up for me?

Alex *and* **Tommy** *bring* **Nina** *into room.*

They put her down.

Tommy   Careful.

Alex   No? Really?

Nina   Those stairs are truly an adventure! You see the dog turds on the fourth floor? They were sculptural, my dears, sculptural – Afternoon to you, Jez.

Jez   Afternoon, sexy.

Tommy   One of your wheels look a bit wonky.

Nina   I slipped down the curb this morning.

Tommy   It just needs a – Hang on!

Pushes wheel into place.

Nina   Oh, my!

Tommy   That should do it!

Link   The Wheelchair Chiropractor.

Jez   That could be a telly series.

Link   'Who's wonky wheel will he fix this week?'

Jez   I'm hooked already.

Nina   What aftershave you wearing, young man?

Tommy   I ... I dunno. It was a present.

Curtis   ... Ocean Desire.

Nina   Ocean Desire! May I have another whiff?

Tommy *leans forward.*

Nina   Mmmm.

Tommy *stands upright.*

Tommy   You … you want us to hunt out some chairs now, Curt?

Alex   Don't bother.

Jez   It's off, apparently.

Nina   Off?

Tommy   Why?

Curtis   This one's taking liberties.

Indicates **Jez**.

Gavin   Tell him to piss off.

Tommy   Gavin's right.

Alex   He goes, I go.

Sarah   She goes, I go.

Nina   She goes, I go.

Curtis   Well. There you have it. Sarah, thanks for asking Nina to help. It's a shame certain friends of yours couldn't keep their bloody noses out of things that don't bloody concern them. And it's an even a bigger shame, now that they *are* here, you won't tell them to go. Nina, thanks for agreeing to help – Tom?

Heads for door.

Nina   Ahhhh! There's something here … I feel it … Secrets!

Curtis *stops.*

Nina   Terrible secrets … Suffocating secrets – Sarah, where's my refreshing libation? Quick! Quick!

Sarah *gets a bottle from the bag she's carrying.*

She gives bottle to **Nina***.*

Nina *drinks.*

Sarah   She's susceptible to atmospheres.

Nina   When I was a child I heard voices. 'Nina,' they said, 'one day you'll be a ballet dancer'. What a sense of humour the spirit world has, eh?

Gavin   That's gin!

Points at **Nina***'s bottle.*

Nina   Slander! I'm a respectable children's librarian!

Gavin   I can smell it from here.

Nina   Well, I can smell you from here but I'm not shouting it from the rooftops.

Tommy   Curt … what d'you wanna do, mate?

Curtis   I … I don't know.

Sarah   Jez has a proposition for you – Don't you, Jez?

Jez   I do?

Sarah   Yes. Jez wants to say he won't write about anything that happens here. He won't take any more photos. Everything that happens here remains … oh, what's the phrase?

Jez   Off the record?

Sarah   Off the record. That goes for all of us. Right?

Nina   Of course.

Sarah   Alex?

Alex   I'm here to support you. That's all.

Sarah   Jez?

Jez   … Okay. But on one condition.

Tommy   No conditions.

Curtis   It's alright, Tom! (*at* **Jez**) Go on.

Jez   You give me an interview. Exclusive. 'How I Changed from Nice Boy To Nazi Boy.'

Curtis   I'm not a Nazi.

Alex   Your nose is growing.

Curtis   I'm bloody *not*!

Tommy   *None* of us are!

Gavin   That's right.

Sarah   Okay, okay. He won't use the word Nazi.

Tommy   Not Fascist either.

Sarah   No words like that. Right, Jez?

Jez   You can describe your political beliefs in whatever way you like. I won't be judgemental.

Gavin   Oh, yeah, and he can trust you, can't he.

Jez   Well, yes, he bloody can actually.

Tommy   You know how I've been described? By the local Gazette? 'A henchman'. My mum was livid.

Jez   I will not misquote or misrepresent anything Curtis says.

Slight pause.

Alex   Ashamed of your views, Curtis?

Curtis   I'm not ashamed of anything.

Gavin   Wayne won't approve this. No way.

Jez   You gonna be bossed around by this Munchkin?

Gavin   Who're you calling a … whatever it was?

Curtis   It might be a chance to explain, Gav. What our policies really are.

Tommy   That's right.

Curtis   How they're for the benefit of everyone.

Alex   So long as they look and think exactly like you.

Curtis   No.

Jez   And you can explain why 'no' in the interview, can't you?

Slight pause.

Curtis *starts to hold out his hand to* **Jez**.

Gavin   Wait! What if they put you on the cover?

Curtis   Eh?

Gavin   It's a magazine for sexual perverts. You want everyone to think you're a secret shirt tail lifter?

Alex   'Shirt tail lifter'?

Jez   It has a quaint charm.

Curtis   You'll make it clear that I'm…you know.

Jez   Fascist but straight. You've got it.

Gavin   Normal! Say he's normal!

Tommy   Nationalist and heterosexual will be fine.

Jez   Okay, okay, whatever.

Curtis   Deal!

Curtis *and* **Jez** *shake hands.*

Alex   You've no idea where that hand was last night.

Curtis *pulls hand away.*

Jez, **Sarah** *and* **Link** *laugh.*

Gavin   It's disgusting – Why's that funny, eh? Where's the bloody joke?

Alex   Perhaps *you're* the bloody joke.

Gavin   Yeah? You think?

Tommy Okay! Chairs! How many we need?

Nina Everyone in the room needs to take part. No spectators allowed. I, as you see, have come fully equipped. One of the bonuses of breaking your back when you're ten. You save a fortune on furniture for the rest of your life.

Tommy So that's … eight.

Curtis Not him.

Points at **Link**.

Alex Why?

Curtis He's sod all to do with any of this.

Gavin (*at* **Link**) You! Out!

Link This is *my* place!

Alex He goes, I go.

Jez She goes, I go.

Sarah Need we carry on?

Curtis Bloody hell, sell tickets, why don't you!

Tommy Okay. Eight chairs.

Curtis Seven.

Tommy But I thought you said –

Curtis Gavin's waiting downstairs.

Gavin Eh? I'm *what*?

Curtis I want you to keep watch.

Gavin For what?

Tommy Just follow instructions, mate.

Gavin Nah, nah, hang on! Immigrants, cripples and perverts can be part of it but *I've* got to wait outside like a … a …

Alex Messy pup?

Gavin   Shut up!

Tommy   All Curtis means is –

Gavin   He can explain himself, I think.

Curtis   I'm just … I'm just nervous Wayne might find out and come here and –

Gavin   How? He thinks we're canvassing the tube stations. 'Our mobiles'll be out of contact for a couple of hours, Wayne.' That's what I told him. What you *told* me to tell him. Why me? Cos he trusts me. Wayne believes everything I decide to tell him.

Curtis   … Look, Gav –

Gavin   Sod the lot of you!

Heads for front door.

Curtis   Tom?!

Tommy   Wait, Gav!

Slight pause.

Gavin   … Well?

Curtis   Mate. I'm sorry. Come here.

Gavin   Why don't *you* come *here*?

Slight pause.

Curtis *goes to* **Gavin**.

Curtis   I wasn't thinking. I've been at my wits end lately. You know that, don't you? None of this would've been possible without you. Would it, Tom, eh?

Tommy   No way.

Gavin   I got a lot of votes pledged this afternoon. I bet Wayne'd be pleased if he knew how good I was getting on.

Curtis   I'll tell him.

Gavin   Perhaps a promotion.

Curtis   Perhaps, yeah.

Gavin   Perhaps *definitely*.

Curtis   … Yes.

Gavin   Chairs!

Curtis   Tommy!

Tommy   Pronto!

Tommy *and* **Gavin** *rush out.*

Nina   Mmm … Ocean Desire!

Alex   With a hint of pig.

Nina   He can wrap his salty rashers round me any day.

Sarah   Nina!

Nina   I know. I despise myself – Curtis! Down to business! Tell me about him!

Curtis   Tom's my best mate.

Nina   Not him. Your dead brother. Jason. That's why we're all here.

Link   So it's your *real* brother! Jason! *He's* the ghost!

Nina   I prefer the word 'spirit', my dear – Sarah, where's my inspirational crystal?

Sarah *gets crystal from bag and gives it to Nina.*

Link   Are you're going to … contact Jason's spirit!

Nina   If I can, yes.

Sarah   Nina made contact with a girl in the library.

Nina   She'd died in a fire there about fifty years ago.

Sarah   She wanted to know the end to a book she'd been reading.

Nina   It was out of print unfortunately.

Link   (*at* **Curtis**) Was your real brother murdered like your real Dad?

Slight pause.

Curtis   I … I don't think I can do this.

Nina   Don't be silly. People's bodys stop working all the time. Don't get all wishy-washy about it.

Curtis   But I can't –

Nina   Listen, sweetie! I've just made my way up an Everest of Dog Turds to get here. I did that because I thought you wanted a séance.

Sarah   He does! – Curt? When I told you about Nina you said you wanted to try this.

Curtis   I did. I *do*.

Nina   Curtis … I know it's hard. You have to open up and talk about things. Things you haven't talked about in years. Perhaps never. It's scary. Right?

Curtis   … Yeah.

Link   You know what my mate says? We only regret the things we *don't* do.

Slight pause.

Curtis   … Okay. No regrets. Let's *do* it.

Nina   Jason! He died six years ago. That right?

Curtis   … Yeah. Six years ago.

Slight pause.

Nina   And? Come on! More!

Link   He did great pictures.

Nina   Eh? What's that?

Curtis   Jason – he painted pictures.

Link   They're in the back room.

Sarah   My God! They're still there!

Rushes for bedroom, then reconsiders, hesitates.

Curtis   I know. Me too.

Sarah   You couldn't …?

Curtis   No.

Sarah   Strange.

Curtis   Yeah.

Sarah   Too …

Curtis   Real.

Sarah   Yeah.

Jez   (*at* **Alex**) You understanding any of this?

Alex   Yeah. Flirt alert.

Sarah   Shut up, Al!

Nina   Dead brother!

Sarah   Jason told him stories.

Jez   From books?

Curtis   No. Jason … he sort of made them up…

Nina   Go on. I'm beginning to feel his karma.

Caresses crystal.

Curtis   When I was a kid – I mean, really young – I used to have trouble getting to sleep. Things used to scare me. Sound of next door's telly. Jason used to tell me stories to calm me down.

Jez   About what?

Curtis   Kings and Queens.

Sarah   Witches and Dragons.

Link   Fairystories.

A distant door gets kicked in.

Dogs bark.

Sarah   He used to mix fantasy up with real stuff – Didn't he, Curt?

Nina   How'd you mean?

Curtis   The stories. He used to put real places and people in them.

Sarah   Your Mum – she became the Queen.

Curtis   Jason – he was the Prince. Or sometimes it was me.

Jez   Prince Curtis!

Nina   Sarah says you couldn't find any photos of him.

Curtis   We lost a lot of stuff when we moved out of here.

Alex   You lost *every* photo of your brother?

Curtis   Not *just* him! All our photos were in one box. We lost the box.

Sarah   You can't blame Curt. He was only twelve at the time.

Nina   It would have been so useful to have some … visual image.

Sarah   That's why I've brought this.

Searches in bag

Curtis   Sarah?

Sarah   The day we went to the fair. Remember?

Takes photo from bag.

Curtis   I didn't know you had that.

Sarah   I've got a few.

Alex   You told me you chucked out everything to do with him.

Sarah   Did I?

Alex   Yes!

Sarah   Then I lied, didn't I!

Holds photo out to **Curtis**.

Slight pause.

Curtis *takes photo.*

Curtis   … Sarah … It's Jason.

Sarah   … You okay?

Curtis   …Yeah.

Jez   Let me see.

Nina   Me! Me!

Takes photo from **Curtis**.

Nina   Oh, Sarah! Look at you!

Jez *and* **Alex** *gather round to look.*

Sarah   I was bit chubby then.

Jez   You were gorgeous

Alex   She *is* gorgeous! A liar, but gorgeous.

Nina   (*at* **Curtis**) You were a midget.

Sarah   He shot up all at once.

Jez   'Shot up all at once.' Oh, Lordy!

Alex   Give it a rest.

Sarah   It's funny … when I think of Jason, he's always so old. Like really grown up. Like my Dad or something. But look at him. He's young. Not much older than we are now.

Nina   When was this taken?

Sarah   The year he died.

Nina   So Jason's … how old?

Sarah   Nineteen. Curtis is twelve. I'm eleven.

Nina   And … cut Jason's hair? Who is it?

Indicates **Curtis**.

Jez   They could be twins.

Looks at **Curtis**.

Nina   And where did you say it was taken?

Sarah   Victoria Park. They used to have a fair there every Spring.

Alex   Still do.

Sarah   But they were so much … *more*, then. Brighter. Louder.

Nina   You're just getting old, my dear. That's all.

Sarah   Jason – he made friends with someone who worked there. Didn't he, Curt?

Curtis   …Yeah, that's right.

Sarah   He had a strange name …

Curtis   A nickname.

Sarah   Yeah … What was it?

Curtis   Something to do with … spinning.

Sarah   Yes! Spinning … round and round …

Curtis   Spiral!

Sarah   Spiral! That's it! He worked on –

Curtis and **Sarah**   – the merry go round!

Sarah   That's why we got all those rides for free.

Curtis   Dolphins!

Sarah   What?

Curtis   The merry go we round. We sat on these big –

Sarah and **Curtis**   – dolphins!

Curtis   Blue dolphins!

Sarah   And the moon, Curt. Remember? It had that big moon above.

Curtis   A mirrorball.

Sarah   Was it?

Curtis   Yeah. It sparkled everywhere.

Sarah   We tried to catch the sparkles – Moonbeams!

Curtis   Moonbeams! That's what we called them!

Sarah   If we catch enough we can turn them into jewels.

Curtis   I've caught one!

Sarah   Me too!

Curtis and **Sarah** *gaze at each other, lost in a bubble of remembrance.*

Pause.

The bubble bursts as –

Tommy *and* **Gavin** *come in holding two chairs each.*

Tommy   Okay. We struck lucky on the floor below.

Sarah   Well done, Tommy.

Tommy   I've wiped them down with a bit of old curtain, but double check before you sit. We'll search another floor.

Sarah   I don't mind standing.

Alex   Nor do I.

Nina   You have to sit. That's the rules. No spectators and everyone sitting round a table and holding hands. The spirits get very stroppy if things are not done properly. And it's me they'll take it out on. Believe me, I don't fancy an ancient aboriginal blowing his didgeridoo in my ear at three in the morning.

Looks at **Tommy**.

Nina   You can blow your didgeridoo in my ear any time, Mr Ocean Desire.

Tommy   Gav!

Heads for door.

Gavin   I'm bloody knackered!

Tommy   You need to get fit!

Tommy *and* **Gavin** *leave.*

Nina   He wiped the chairs – Oh, what a considerate love!

Sarah   Nina!

Nina   (*at* **Curtis**) Your brother's death!

Pause.

Come on, come on.

Curtis   Give me … give me a second. I need to get it … into some kind of order. You don't live life as a story, do you? You live it as life. The stories happen later.

Jez   Oh, that's good.

Takes notebook from bag and scribbles in it.

Sarah   Off the record! Remember?

Holds out her hand.

Jez   But it's a gem!

Sarah   You gave your word!

Jez *gives her the notebook.*

Sarah   Curtis?

Curtis   Jason had been looking after me since our Dad died.

Nina   Which was …?

Curtis   Dad died when –

Jez   It happened when Curtis was eleven. Must have been the year before that photo … (*at* **Curtis**) Sorry. It's *your* story.

Curtis   My Mum … she went off the rails a bit.

Sarah   It was clinical depression, Curt.

Link   My mate gets that. He says it's like falling into a dark pit.

Sarah   It is.

Link   Once I touched his hand and he cried.

Curtis   Mum started bringing stray dogs into the flat. She wasn't eating properly … Wasn't washing … Me and Jason – we were so scared for her.

Sarah   But your Mum got better as soon as she met Mr Avalon.

Curtis   Oh, yeah.

Nina   How long after your Dad dying did she meet Mr Avalon?

Curtis   Nine months.

Jez   Where did they meet?

Curtis   In the doctor's surgery. They were both waiting to see the same doctor. They started talking and – Wham! Love at first sight, I guess. Mum – she changed over night.

Sarah   She was her old self again.

Curtis   *Better* than her old self. It was brilliant. Jason was over the moon. He could get on with his life now. He'd put so much on hold to look after me. He didn't apply for art school. And he could've done. Mr Avalon knew that Jason wanted to travel so he gave him some money to go anywhere in the world. Explore. It was a dream come true for Jason. He couldn't stop talking about it. Remember, Sarah?

Sarah   Do I!? All those maps. That big compass.

Jez   Where did he go?

Curtis   The Columbian jungle.

Link   I'd love to go there!

Curtis   Jason wanted to see the Lost City. God, he was so excited. He was gonna hike it. More of an adventure, he said. He talked me through the route night after night. The Sierra Nevada Mountains. We took him to the airport. Me, Mum, Mr Avalon and Wayne. Jason was crying buckets. He kept saying, 'I've got to do this, Curt. I'll miss you. But I've gotta go.' I was crying too. I'd never cried like that before. Not even when dad died. I hung onto Jason's jacket. I didn't wanna let go. Mr Avalon said, 'Don't worry. You'll see him again.' They had to pull me away from him. I was screaming. 'Don't go, brov! Don't leave me!' Mr Avalon told Jason to run. Jason went through the checkout … he turned round to look at me … He was crying … then he … he disappeared …

Visibly distressed, he goes to balcony.

A distant door is kicked in.

Dogs bark

Jez *sneakily aims camera at* **Curtis**.

Sarah   Jez!

Jez *looks at* **Sarah**.

Sarah *holds her hand out for camera.*

Slight pause.

Jez *gives camera to* **Sarah**.

Jez   Spoilsport.

Sarah   Hypocrite.

Nina   (*at* **Sarah**) Get loverboy back. I need to know more.

Sarah   *I* can tell you. And he's *not* loverboy.

Alex   No?

Sarah   No!

Nina   … Okay. So Jason has disappeared through the checkout and flown off to … where was it again?

Link   Columbian jungle.

Jez   The Lost City.

Sarah   There were a few postcards from him. Fantastic pictures on them. Flowers big as … that armchair. Monkeys. Sunsets you wouldn't believe. The last postcard said not to worry if it goes quiet for a while as he's about to enter the jungle and, as far as he knew, there weren't many post offices along the way. We all laughed at that.

Link   And *did* it go quiet?

Sarah   Oh, yes. A few weeks went by. A month. Two months. Not a word from him. No one worried. All Curtis talked about was Jason coming back. 'I hope he's back for the wedding. He's gotta be here for the wedding.'

Nina   That's the wedding of Mr Avalon and Curtis's mum?

Sarah   Yeah, she'd moved in with him.

Nina   In sin! What fun!

Sarah   The council had started moving everyone out of this place by then so … well, I suppose it was the obvious thing to do. And Mr Avalon's politics weren't so … focused as they are now. I remember he used to talk about the Blitz spirit and land of hope and glory. We all thought he was a bit of a joke. But I do remember one time … I forget when exactly. But it was early on. I was sitting in the living room with Curtis. Mr Avalon was spouting off about how his wife – his first wife – had had to wait ages for hospital treatment. 'It's the immigrants swamping the national health,' he kept saying. 'They killed my wife.'

Nina   What did she die of?

Sarah   Some cancer thing.

Jez   Leukaemia.

Sarah   That's it. Wayne once told me his Dad hardly ever visited his first wife. Mr Avalon hated hospitals. It was all left up to Wayne. Must've been terrible for him. She died in the same month as Curtis's Dad. It's what bonded Mr Avalon and Curtis's Mum so quick. They kept talking about fate and stuff. You know? Both mourning the death of a spouse.

Jez   Both blossoming Fascists.

Sarah   No! *Not* Curtis's Mum

Jez   But she *is*!

Sarah   You didn't see her after the murder.

Alex   What's *that* got to do with it?

Sarah   She was a wreck, Alex. Neighbours pointing at her. Kids calling her names. I don't blame her for clinging onto anything that could save her. I'm not saying I agree with it. But if you ask me if I'd prefer to see her like she is now or how she was after the murder I'd take now any day. I grew up with her. I lived three floors below. This was like a second home to me.

Alex   Perhaps you see it different after you've dated a Fascist.

Sarah   I did *not* date a Fascist!

Alex   You forgotten that speech?

Sarah   And that's when it ended! But until that moment I didn't … I didn't realise … oh, it all crept up so slowly.

Alex   I saw it coming a mile off.

Sarah   You saw a boy! That's all! Politics had nothing to do with it!

Alex   What's *that* supposed to mean?

Sarah   You know!

Alex   No! *You* tell *me*!

Nina   Let's get back to the task in hand, shall we?

Slight pause.

Sarah, my dear?

Sarah   … There was a telegram. It said Jason had gone missing.

Nina   In the jungle?

Sarah   Yes.

Nina   And then?

Sarah   It's hard to … remember the order of things.

Jez   They found a skull or something, didn't they?

Sarah   That's right. Thanks, Jez. Mr Avalon got a letter. It said a skull had been found by the edge of a river.

Link   Just a skull?

Nina   Did they carry out tests?

Sarah   Yes. Mr Avalon showed Curtis every bit of information he got. The tests were one hundred per cent certain.

Jez   Jason was toast.

Link   But to find just a skull? What could've happened to him?

Sarah   No one was sure. It was assumed he was walking along this ledge by a river and he … he must have slipped and fallen in and … something happened … a speedboat…

Jez   Eaten by crocodiles.

Sarah   Don't, Jez!

Nina   It's a possibility, my dear.

Sarah   I just hope it was quick, that's all. Whatever happened, I hope he didn't suffer.

Tommy *comes in with two chairs.*

Tommy   Okay. Nearly there. Gav's searching the lower floors for some more.

Nina   Look at those arms. Let me feel your muscles, Mr Ocean Desire … Come on! I don't bite.

Feels **Tommy***'s arms.*

Nina   Let's skip the small talk. How'd you fancy a date with a mermaid? If you kiss me – who knows? I might start to walk and dance the rumba.

Slight pause.

Tommy   … Where's Curtis?

Sarah *indicates balcony.*

Tommy   Should I …?

Sarah *shakes head.*

Sarah   Perhaps you can tell Nina about the ghost, Tom. The first time Curtis saw it.

Nina   Were you with him, my dear?

Tommy   Yeah. I'd been at the –

Sarah   Hang on – Jez?

Holds out her hands for voice recorder.

Jez   But I'm not –

Sarah   I don't trust you.

Jez *gives the recorder to* **Sarah***.*

Sarah   Go on, Tom.

Tommy   I'd been boxing at the York Hall. Curtis came. Never misses.

Nina   I bet you look gorgeous in your shorts.

Jez   In the showers!

Nina   Be still my heart!

Sarah   You win the fight, Tom?

Tommy   A knockout!

Sarah and **Nina**   Yesss!

Tommy   We went for an Indian afterwards.

Alex   Oh, the joys of multi-culturalism, eh?

Sarah   Not now, Alex! – Tom?

Tommy   … We got back to Curtis's place about midnight. We went up to his room. We were playing some music. Curtis got up to pull the curtains and – I heard him gasp! I looked up at him. I thought he was going to faint. I said, 'What's up, mate? He said, 'Tom! Look!' He pointed to the other side of the road. 'It's Jason! Jason's ghost!' I looked out the window.

Nina   What did you see?

Tommy   The other side of the road.

Jez   What about Jason?

Tommy   That's what I mean. All I saw was the other side of the road. No ghost.

Nina   But *Curtis* had seen it.

Tommy   Oh, yeah. You should've seen him. He kept saying, 'I've just seen Jason! I've just seen Jason.' He wanted me to stay the night. I said, 'Sure.' I've got my own zed bed in his room. I kept awake and made sure he was safe.

Sarah   Oh, Tom.

Nina   How far away is the other side of the road?

Jez   Twenty yards.

Nina   And is it well lit?

Tommy   Not really.

Nina   So why's Curtis so sure he saw Jason's ghost?

Gavin *enters – breathless and sweating – with two chairs.*

Tommy   Well done, Gav.

Gavin   Yeah, yeah.

Nina   Can you smell – oh, Dopey's walked something in.

Gav   Eh? What?

Tommy   Check your shoes, mate.

Gavin *checks his shoes.*

Jez   Ugh!

Alex   You smell like your politics.

Gavin   Shut up!

Nina   Sarah, where's my eau de toilet?

Sarah   Here, Neen.

Gets it from **Nina***'s bag.*

Nina *sprays herself.*

The others are all laughing at **Gavin***.*

Alex   Messy pup!

Jez   You should stay outside.

Gavin   Shut up! Shut up!

Link   It's supposed to be lucky.

Gavin *punches* **Link** *hard.*

Link *stumbled back and falls.*

General cries etc from everyone.

Jez *rushes at* **Gavin***.*

Jez   You bloody bastard.

Gets **Gavin** *in arm lock.*

Gavin   I'll fucking kill you.

Jez   Come on, then! *Come on*!

Gavin *can't free himself.*

Jez   I'll snap your fucking arm off!

Curtis *has rushed in.*

Curtis   What's going on!

Sarah   Gavin hit Link.

Gavin   He was laughing at me – Ahhh!

Jez *has twisted Gavin's arm.*

Link *is on his feet.*

His nose is bleeding.

Sarah   We were *all* laughing at you! Wanna hit me too? Come on!

Nina   What about me? I'm more your size!

Curtis   (*at* **Jez**) Let him go.

Slight pause.

Jez *lets go of* **Gavin**.

Link   I'm gonna get Zak. You'll be sorry.

Gavin   Get him! He don't scare me!

Link *runs out of flat.*

Alex   Link!

Sarah   Link!

Jez   Come back, mate.

Gavin   Bloody vagrant. Should've cleared off in the first place.

Jez *steps towards* **Gavin**.

Gavin *steps back.*

Jez   Pig!

Curtis   Get out!

Gavin   (*at* **Jez**) You heard!

Curtis   Not him! *You!*

Gavin   Wh-what?

Tommy   Curt?

Curtis   I know what I'm doing! – You've been warned, Gav. Out!

Gavin   Warned? *Me?*

Steps towards **Curtis**.

Tommy *stands in front of* **Gavin**.

Tommy   Careful, Gavin.

Gavin   (*at* **Curtis**) I've heard you talking. In the gym. You don't see me. Oh, no. I'm just there to collect your spit in a bucket. But I've got ears.

Tommy   So what?

Gavin   So what? 'I'm being haunted, Tom.' 'I can't sleep, Tom.' 'Can you get something to calm me down, Tom?' Whimpering like a bloody baby.

Tommy   That's enough!

Gavin   Know what I think? You're losing it. Men in white coats'll come along and cart you off to the loony bin. That's where you belong. Because I tell you this. You're a liability to the party. Hear me? A liability!

Curtis   Get. Out!

Slight pause.

Get out!

Gavin *leaves.*

Pause.

Curtis   Come on. Let's get on with it. Quick!

Nina   You're sure it was Jason's ghost you saw?

Curtis   Positive.

Nina   Why?

Curtis   The jacket.

Nina   What jacket?

Sarah   The sparkle jacket.

Curtis   That's what we called it.

Sarah   We were only kids.

Curtis   Jason was given a jacket.

Sarah   A present.

Curtis   Spiral!

Sarah   What?

Curtis   I remember now. It was a present from Spiral!

Sarah   You're right! Oh, God.

Nina   There's lots of jackets, my darlings.

Sarah   Oh, not like this, Neen.

Curtis   It'd had those silver stud things on it.

Sarah   All over.

Curtis   Swirling shapes.

Sarah   Some of them were coloured.

Curtis   Like jewels.

Sarah   It was beautiful.

Curtis   Weighed a ton.

Sarah   There was painting on it too.

Curtis   Round the collar.

Sarah   On the back.

Curtis   Sleeves

Nina   What of?

Curtis   Dolphins.

Sarah   Moons.

Curtis   All done by hand.

Sarah   Unique, Nina, unique.

Curtis   Jason was wearing it at the airport. When I said goodbye.
The jacket I was clutching onto – Nina, it's my brother's ghost
I saw. I *know* it was. And I've seen him three times since then.
Twice more outside the house. And once outside the community
hall after Wayne's speech. The ghost was standing in the estate
opposite. It was in the shadows. I saw the jacket sparkle. I pushed
through the crowds to chase after it. Some people got knocked to
the floor. Local press took photos. Wayne and Stacey did their nut.

Nina   Did you tell them about the ghost?

Curtis   Wayne and Stacey? Jesus, no. Tommy's the only one.

Nina   The turd foot dwarf seems to know.

Tommy   That was an accident.

Curtis   He heard me and Tommy talking.

Tommy   We *had* to involve him.

Curtis   I hated him knowing – Didn't I, Tom?

Tommy   You did, mate.

Curtis   But there was no choice. I had to go ahead with … what
we're doing now. If I didn't … It's been doing my head in.

Tommy   His hands wouldn't stop shaking.

Sarah   They still are.

Tommy   That's why I phoned you.

Alex   Yeah. Why *her* exactly?

Tommy   Because my mate needed help.

Alex   Well, *she's* my mate and I don't appreciate *you* digging up –

Tommy   I don't give a toss! I'd do anything for him.

Alex   Well, I'd do anything for her and she don't need you coming along and –

Curtis   Don't pick on him!

Sarah   Stop it! Stop it! I *wanted* to come, Alex! I told you. I didn't want to turn a corner one day and … see him when I wasn't ready! Okay? Now, put a sock in it!

Nina   Cover the windows! Chairs round the table! It's time to talk to the dead!

They start to find ways of covering the windows.

Most of the boards can be put back in place.

A blanket is used for the balcony window.

Much noisy activity and bustle as –

Nina   Hang it over the curtain rail!…That's it! Just lean that board against the – Yes! Good! There's still light there! … That'll have to do … The chairs! Come on!

The chairs have been put in place.

They are gathering round the table.

Nina   Sit!

Curtis *sits in between* **Nina** *and* **Sarah**.

Alex *swops places with* **Jez** *so she can be on the other side of* **Sarah**.

This means **Tommy** *is now sitting next to* **Jez**.

Nina   Hands!

Tommy *hesitates at holding* **Jez**'s *hand.*

The others watch.

Slight pause.

Tommy *holds* **Jez**'s *hand.*

Nina   Spirits! Hear our cry! We come in search of Jason. Brother to Curtis. He passed into your world six years ago. Please help us, oh, spirits. Something is troubling Jason. I have sensed secrets. Please, spirits. Guide Jason to us.

Nothing happens.

Slight pause.

Nina   Spirits! Please … Guide Jason to us!

Nothing happens.

Slight pause.

Jez   My belly's rumbling.

Sarah   Shhh!

Nina   Jason … hear us.

Sarah   It's … it's getting colder.

Jez   It's not.

Alex   It *is*.

Tommy   I can feel it too.

Nina   It's the spirits.

Sarah   You feel it?

Curtis   Yes.

Tommy   It's like the North Pole.

Jez   … Oh, God.

Pulls back

Nina   Don't lose the circle!

They touch hands again.

Nina   Jason!

Sarah   I've got goose bumps.

Alex   Me too.

Jez   I'm freezing.

Tommy   Curt?

Curtis   I'm alright – Sarah?

Sarah   I'm okay.

Nina   I … feel something. Yes … oh, yes. Something is getting closer…closer… Jason! …

Pause.

Zak *rushes in! He is twenty-two years old and wearing jeans and a jacket decorated with silver studs and paint (exactly as described by* **Curtis** *and* **Sarah***).*

The others scream, cry out, jump up etc.

Zak   Where is he?

Jez   Jesus!

Zak   (*at* **Jez**) Was it you? Eh?

Alex   Leave him alone.

Sarah   Tom!

Tommy   Oi!

Zak *approaches* **Tommy***.*

Zak   It was you, wasn't it!

Tommy   Me *what*? – Piss off!

Pushes **Zak** *back.*

Zak   Come on, then!

Tommy   Yeah?

Zak   Yeah!

Link *runs in, breathless.*

Link   Zak! Zak!

Looks round room.

It's … okay. It's … it's not any of these – Where's he gone? The bastard who hit me?

Nina   There was a … a disagreement, my dear.

Jez   A blazing row!

Alex   Gavin's not here, Link.

Link   Lucky for him. My mate was gonna teach him a lesson – Weren't you, Zak?

Jez   This is … Zak?

Link   My mate, yeah.

Nina   No ghosts this time.

Sarah   But … the jacket – Curt?

Curtis   I know, I know.

Hurriedly knocks boards from windows etc.

Setting sunlight fills the room.

Slight pause.

Zak *is gazing at* **Curtis**.

Sarah   That jacket – It's Jason's!

Alex   It can't be.

Sarah   It is! It *is*!

Curtis   Where did you get it?

Link   He's had it ages. Since before I met him.

Curtis   Tell me where you got the bloody jacket?

Sarah   Did someone give it to you?

Curtis   You better tell me.

Tommy   Tell him.

Zak starts packing bags.

Zak   Link! Come on!

Link   Zak? … What you doing?

Zak   We're going.

Link   Going? Why?

Zak   Just pack up our stuff.

Link   But I thought we liked it here.

Zak   I did but … Come on! I can't explain!

Nina   Jason gave you that jacket, didn't he?

Zak freezes.

Jez   Oh, Lordy.

Sarah   Is it true, Zak?

Nina   Oh, it's true. (at **Zak**) Right, my dear?

Link   Zak?

Zak resumes packing.

Sarah   Did you … did you meet him in the jungle?

Link   Zak ain't been to no jungle.

Nina   Is that true?

Link   He's never been abroad – Have you?

Zak   You helping me pack or what?

Link *starts packing bags.*

Nina   Do you know how Jason died?

Zak *freezes.*

Jez   Oh, Lordy.

Alex   He knows.

Sarah   Oh, Curt.

Zak *picks up bag and heads for the front door.*

Link   Hang on! The book!

Zak *gets book.*

Zak *and* **Link** *head for the door –*

Sarah   No! You can't go!

Nina   Please stay!

Sarah   Curt! *Curt!*

Curtis   Don't go!

Zak *freezes.*

Curtis   You can't go and … not tell me! Don't think you'll upset me. You won't. I've imagined so many things about how Jason died. Each one worse than the last. No matter how bad it was I'd rather … I'd rather just know. Zak. I need to know what happened to my brother … Please.

Zak *turns to face* **Curtis**.

Zak   I … I can't tell you.

Curtis   Why?

Zak   I made a promise.

Cutis   To who?

Slight pause.

Nina   To Jason?

Zak   ... Yeah.

Turns to leave again –

Nina   Jason didn't die in the jungle, did he?

Zak *freezes.*

Jez   Oh, lordy.

Curtis   Of *course* he died in the bloody jungle. What you going on about?

Nina   Your brother went to the jungle with that jacket, you said. Now it's here on Zak and he's never been abroad. *You* work it out.

Curtis   Jason went to the airport. I waved goodbye to him.

Sarah   But the jacket's here, Curt! Look!

Curtis   The authorities sent photos of where my brother went missing. Sarah, you saw them. My Dad showed us.

Sarah   *Not* your Dad! *Avalon!*

Curtis   They sent cremated remains, for chrissakes. We threw them from the roof of this place. Jason's dead! Six years ago. In the Columbian jungle ... Perhaps that's not his jacket.

Sarah   You *know* it is.

Jez   Did Jason ... did he fake his own death?

Zak   Whatever he did ... he did it because ...

Sarah   W*hat*, Zak? *What?*

Nina   You've got to tell us, my dear.

Jez   We'll keep on guessing and guessing till you do.

Nina   You *want* to tell us, don't you!

Zak   Of *course* I want to! But I can't ... I ... can't.

Link   You're upsetting him. Leave him alone.

Nina   Why did you come here, Zak?

Zak   Because … because I wanted to feel close to … someone again. To see the things they grew up with … To see the people they spoke about and … I can't explain it. You have to … love someone…and lose them. Lose someone so special it's like … gravity going. Nothing to hold you on the planet any more. You won't understand that.

Sarah   Oh, I do.

Curtis Me too.

Nina *wheels closer to* **Zak**.

Nina   Listen, my dear. A secret like you've got – it's like a piranha in your belly. And piranhas are ravenous things. Their little jaws keep nibbling and nibbling. In the end, they'll eat so much of you there'll be nothing left. What's the cure? Spit the piranha out. Here! Now!

Zak   But … but I promised. I promised Jason … I would never …

Sarah   Why don't you do what Jason used to do. Tell us a story.

Link   Yeah! A fairy story!

Nina   Oh, *very* good.

Jez   Of course! After all, a fairy story – that's not real life, is it?

Alex   Not real life at all.

Nina   And if we … well, if we *deduce* things from that story …

Sarah   Well, that's not Zak's fault, is it?

Nina   He wouldn't've broke any promise.

Sarah   None at all.

Jez   None.

Alex   No way.

Curtis Please, Zak … I need to know.

Slight pause.

Link Show them what you can do, Zak. What *we* can do! Street entertainers supreme! Come on! Showtime!

Has climbed up on table.

Ladies and gentleman! Roll up, roll up! Spare us a few minutes of your time and enter a world of enchantment and wonder.

Nina Very good!

Wheels closer to table.

Link We bring you stories! Fantasy. Thriller. Thriller-fantasy. Comedy-weepie-fantasy! Zak here will spin a tale of surprise and magic before your very eyes. Nothing is prepared. Just call out three things and Zak will spin a web of a story to take your breath away. Come on! Don't be shy. This is an experience not to be missed. Three things. Anything you like … Who'll gimme the first?

Others are gathering round.

Nina A Prince called Jason!

Link First thing! A Prince called Jason! Next?

Sarah A jacket that sparkles.

Link Second thing! A jacket that sparkles! Oh, this is going to be a challenge, O! Storyteller. One more!

Curtis … A death!

Link … Okay! Zak, O! Great Storyteller! Your storytelling challenge has been set. A story with a Prince called Jason. A jacket that sparkles. And a death. Tell us this story, O! plot-weaving wizard.

Jumps off table.

Slight pause.

Slowly, **Zak** *gets up onto table.*

Others are sitting round table like an audience.

The setting sunlight is now very intense.

For a while **Zak** *does nothing.*

Then, abruptly, it's showtime –

Zak There was once a King and Queen.

Link We're off!

Zak The King and Queen had a son. Prince Jason!

Link The first thing! Well done, O! Storyteller.

Zak One day Prince Jason looked out of the window and saw everything had turned white. Snow. He'd never seen it before. He rushed outside to play.

Link Where did he go, O! Storyteller?

Zak Prince Jason went to the forest, my inquisitive Apprentice. He climbed trees and knocked icicles from branches. He made snowmen. He made snow angels. He played all day. When he got home his lips had turned bright blue and he lay on his bed as motionless as a statue. A layer of frost covered his skin. The King and Queen started a big log fire in his room but, no matter how hot the room got, the layer of frost remained on Prince Jason.

Link Something is wrong with the Prince! Oh, we're captivated already! What happens next! Tell us, O! Storyteller!

Zak A Witch!

Link Of course! Why?

Zak The King went to a Witch and asked her to cure whatever was ailing the Prince. The Witch said, 'Prince Jason has snow in the bones. There is only one cure I know of. You must go to the Wild Orchard at the edge of the Kingdom and pick him some lemons from the tallest tree'.

Link Lemons? To make ... a lemon drink!

The others are beginning to visibly react now.

They recognise the death of Curtis's dad in the story.

They glance at **Curtis**.

Zak   But there was something the Witch forgot to warn the King about – Come on, Apprentice!

Link   What did the Witch forget to warn the King about?

Zak   The Dragon, my ever-attentive Apprentice. The Dragon that protected the Wild Orchard. And when this Dragon saw the King picking lemons it swooped down on the King. The King cried out. The Dragon raised its claws and … stabbed the King.

Link   The King's dead?!

Zak   The King's *wounded*! He walked all the way back to the castle.

Link   Leaving a trail of blood in the snow.

Zak   The King climbed the steps in tower.

Link   A rose petal of blood on every step.

Zak   The King got to the top of the tower. The King went to Prince Jason's room. The King gave the magic lemons to his sick son.

Link   And that's when the King fell down dead.

Zak   In front of his son!

Link   And what about Prince Jason? Was he cured of snow in the bones?

Zak   Yes. But – oh, the guilt Prince Jason felt, my Apprentice. The King is dead all because Prince Jason got snow in the bones. And now – oh, more guilt for the Prince.

Link   What, O! Storyteller?

Zak   The King's death sent the Queen mad. She started to bring wolves into the castle. She cried, 'My precious wolves. They are all I need.'

Everyone is beginning to react more and more.

Lots of glances, tiny gasps, nods.

Lots of looks towards **Curtis***.*

Curtis *is looking increasingly agitated.*

Zak   Prince Jason couldn't bear to see the Queen so distressed. He went on long walks. He walked to parts of the Kingdom he'd never been to before. One day he found himself by the edge of a – oh, look!

Link   What?

Zak   It's a lagoon. The water is smooth as glass.

Link   I see it!

Zak   The Prince sits beside it. A young man comes up and sits beside the Prince and says, 'You know, there's a legend about this lagoon. It says that dolphins will appear whenever two people who are in love with each other are reflected in the water.'

Link   What's this young man called, O! Storyteller?

Zak   He's called … Spiral. Prince Jason and Spiral sit by the edge of the lagoon and talk. They talk all day and into the night. They talk like they have never talked to anyone before. Like they've known each other all their lives. Then they hold each other. Then they kiss each other. They look at their reflections on the surface of the lagoon. And … dolphins appear.

Slight pause.

Back to the Queen!

Link   Wolves!

Zak   No!

Link   No?

Zak   The Queen has met a New King now. And the Queen is in love with this New King. They plan to get married.

Link   Stop press! Queen to marry New King!

Zak   But there's a problem.

Link   Tell us!

Zak   The lagoon. Moonlight. Stars. Prince Jason says to Spiral.
'I've never felt like this towards … anyone. You've made me feel
lots of new things. Up until now my life has been in neat boxes.
All of them ordered and labelled. But you … you have come
along and blown all the boxes apart. I want us to get as close as
possible in all possible ways.' And Spiral says, 'I feel the same.
That's why I have made you a gift to celebrate what we have
created together …'

Link   What is it, O! Storyteller?

Zak   'Once a month the dolphins collect moonlight from the
surface of the lagoon. This moonlight it the most precious thing
in the whole world. I have woven it into this garment, my Prince.
See how it sparkles. Please put on … It is called Moonfleece!'

Link   The second thing! A jacket that sparkles! Well done, O!
Storyteller!

Zak   Many thanks, sweet Apprentice – But aren't you missing
something?

Link   What?

Zak   I mentioned a problem.

Link   Forgive me, O! Storyteller. What is this problem you
mentioned?

Zak   The New King says to the Queen, 'There must be a reason
why our lives went so wrong.' The Queen says, 'I agree, but
what could it have been?' The New King says, 'Well, my wife
died when the moon was full.' The Queen says, 'I think the moon
was full when my husband was killed too.' The New King says,
'That's it! Don't you see? The moon is to blame for everything.'
The Queen says, 'Goodness! I've been so blind.' The New King
says, 'We'll create a new kingdom without anything to do with the

moon! People who like the moon will be banished. All references
to the moon will be taken out of the books. If the moon shines at
night people must close their windows. If they happen to catch
sight of it they must call it nasty names. And we will name this
new kingdom after me. We will call it Avalon!' – You see the
problem, sweet Apprentice?

Slight pause.

Apprentice!?

Link   Yes. I see the problem. Prince Jason is wearing Moonfleece
in a Kingdom called Avalon where the moon is despised.

Curtis *is getting very agitated.*

Sarah *is trying to calm him.*

Zak   Ahhhhh!!!

Link   What's happening now?

Zak   I'm the Queen.

Link   What's happened, Queen?

Zak   I've just seen Prince Jason.

Link   And he's wearing Moonfleece!

Zak   'What are you wearing, my son?' 'Moonfleece.' 'Moon!
Haven't you heard anything King Avalon has been saying?'
'That's crazy talk, Mum.' 'Shhh! King Avalon will hear you.'
'Too late, my love. I heard everything!' 'I'm sure he didn't mean
it.' 'I do, Mum!' 'Take it off, Jason!' 'No, Avalon! I like it!' 'It's
disgusting!' 'It's not!' 'Then you can't be part of this new family.'
'Please, son. Do it for me!' 'I'd do anything for you, Mum! You
know I would! But I must wear Moonfleece! Moonfleece is what
I am!' 'Listen to me, you selfish boy! I have ambitions! Plans for
my future kingdom are taking shape. Someone like you could ruin
everything for me. I can't have you around. I will you give a chest
of gold to start a new life elsewhere. We will tell everyone here
that you were killed in an accident. A fatal accident. I will fake all
the necessary documents. You will never show your face in this

Kingdom again. You must never make contact with your Mum. Or your younger brother.'

Link   Younger brother?

Zak   Prince Jason has a younger brother. Haven't I mentioned that? What a bloody oversight. His name's Prince Curtis. And Prince Curtis adores Prince Jason. You remember when their real Dad – the old King – had been killed? Prince Jason took care of Prince Curtis after that. And now their new Dad, this Avalon, is telling Jason he must go away and never see his Mum or Curtis again. And Jason says, 'If that's what my Mum wants, I'll do it. But only if it's what *she* wants. Do you want me to disappear, Mum? *Do* you?'

Curtis *is murmuring 'no … no…' now.*

His distress and agitation are becoming uncontrollable.

Others are trying to restrain and calm him.

Zak   Ask me what the Mum replies, Apprentice.

Slight pause.

Ask me!

Link   What … what does Mum reply?

Zak *jumps off table and faces* **Curtis**.

Zak   … 'Yes.'

Curtis   No!

Zak   Jason couldn't bear to see your Mum upset again! He'd seen it after your real Dad died. Jason wanted her to be happy!

Curtis   I waved him off at the airport!

Zak   And so he went to the jungle. He sent you cards.

Curtis   Yes!

Zak   But he came back.

Curtis   I'm not listening!

Zak   Avalon faked the whole thing. Documents. Human remains.

Curtis   Shut up!

Zak   Jason was back in this country all the time, Curtis. Travelling from place to place.

Curtis   I don't believe you!

Zak   I met him two years ago. In Cornwall. We lived together.

Curtis   No! No!

Zak   I was happy. But Jason wasn't. He wanted to come to you and tell you the whole story.

Curtis   Then why didn't he?

Zak   Your Mum. He didn't want you feeling bad things about her.

Curtis   Shut up!

Zak   That's why he made me promise. No matter what happened to him. I must *never* find you. *Never* tell you the truth.

Curtis   Shut up! Shut up!

Zak   But now I have! And you know what? I'm glad!

Curtis   I'm warning you!

Zak   Curtis … The people you love … your family – They've all lied to you!

Curtis   NO!

Launches himself at **Zak**.

Curtis   I don't believe it! I don't believe it!

Zak *and* **Curtis** *struggle.*

Tommy   Don't, mate! Don't!

Pulls **Curtis** *off* **Zak**.

Curtis   Let me go! Let go!

Struggles with **Tommy**.

Tommy   Stop it, mate. Please! Stop it!

Zak *and* **Link** *go out to the balcony.*

Slowly, **Curtis**'s *anger is spent.*

He is like a clockwork toy running down as –

Curtis   I don't believe it … Sarah? You hear what he said?
Jason wouldn't leave me … My Mum – she wouldn't agree …
You *know* my Mum, Sarah … Tom? You know her! … My Mum
wouldn't … my Mum wouldn't … I *know* her … I know … I
know … my Mum … my Mum … my Mum …

Slight pause.

It's almost dark outside now.

Wayne *rushes in. He is twenty-one years old and wearing a
dove-grey suit.*

Wayne   Phew! Those stairs! … Dark and smelly or what, eh?
Hello, everyone. Wayne. Wayne Avalon. Nice to see you all. Hello
… Pleasure … Sarah! You look well. Hair's different. Suits you.

Points at **Nina**.

Wayne   Library! Right? Like your dress. Greens your colour.
Tom, I'm a bit out of condition, mate. I need a Tom special work
out.

Goes to **Curtis**.

Wayne   Brov! What is all this? You're worrying us sick, buddy.

Stacey *rushes in. She is twenty years old and wearing a light-grey
skirt and white blouse. She is holding* **Gavin**'s *lighter.*

Stacey   Oh, those stairs! Could barely see a thing! Where's that
Gavin got to – Gav?!

Wayne   Leave him!

Stacey   But I've got his lighter.

Wayne   Then he should've kept up with you! – Stace! Look who's had her hair done!

Stacey   Sarah! Oh, sweetheart! You look brilliant. And that dress! You've lost weight. I hate you. Only joking. Hello, everyone … Pleasure … Hi … You can really feel autumn coming in now, can't you, eh?

Points at **Nina**.

Stacey   Library! Right? Green's really your colour. I think it's wonderful the way you make the most of yourself.

Wayne   Stace?

Indicates **Curtis**.

Stacey   Oh, sweetheart. We've been worried sick.

Wayne   I told him.

Stacey *goes to* **Curtis** *and holds his hand.*

Stacey   You're trembling sweetheart. Wayne, he's burning up.

Wayne   Let's get you home, buddy.

Wayne *heads for door.*

Stacey *tugs at* **Curtis**'*hand.*

Curtis *doesn't move.*

Stacey   Oh, sweetheart. What is it?

Wayne   Curt? What's up?

Stacey   This place is getting gloomier by the second. Come on.

Nina   He hasn't heard the end of the story.

Wayne   Eh? What story's this?

Zak *and* **Link** *are now coming in from the balcony.*

Nina   These two handsome boys here. They're street entertainers. They've been telling us a story.

Sarah   With three things in.

Nina   Things we chose.

Stacey   Oh, how cute!

Sarah   So far we've only had two of the three things.

Tommy   That's right, yeah.

Nina   I'm sure when we've heard the whole story all of us will want to go.

Stacey   Oh, you *must* hear the end, Curt. Of course you must. It'll drive you crazy if you don't. Remember when your mum recorded that murder mystery for us, Wayne. And we sat up late one night to watch it. And just as we were about to find out who done it the screen went all fuzzy and the snooker came on? Ooo, we could've killed your Mum, couldn't we. Joke.

Wayne   Do you mind if we listen on?

Stacey   Oh, I'm sure they wouldn't.

Nina   The more the merrier.

Wayne   That's great. Thank you.

Stacey   Yes, thank you.

Slight pause.

Link   O! Storyteller …

Stacey   Ooo! Goosebumps. Look!

Link   One thing remains to be woven into the fabric of your tale. Please put us out of our misery and tell us …

Slight pause.

Zak *goes to speak but can't.*

He shakes his head.

Wayne   Something wrong?

Nina   Sore throat.

Stacey   You need a good gargle with lemon juice and honey. You put it in hot water as hot as you can bear and –

Makes gargling noise.

Slight pause.

Link   I think … *I* can finish it.

Nina   *You* know the end?

Link   I … I think I do, yeah. Zak? It's the … the friend you told me about. Right?

Zak *nods.*

Nina   Go on, then, brave Apprentice.

Moonlight is now filling the room.

Link   The Prince … he travels for many years. Until he reaches a place where land ends and sea begins. The Prince sits on the beach and thinks of his old kingdom. He misses it so much but knows he can never go back. But he made a promise to the Queen – is this right, Zak?

Zak *nods.*

Link   He made a promise to the Queen and the Prince would never do anything to upset the Queen. He saw the Queen very upset once before, you see. And he couldn't bear to see her like that again.

Stacey   Question! Why can't he go back exactly?

Link   The Prince loves moonlight.

Nina   And moonlight has been banished from the kingdom.

Wayne   How can you banish moonlight?

Stacey   It's a fairytale, silly.

Link   And then the Prince sees dolphins swimming out in the ocean. They seem to be calling his name. The Prince walks into the water. The dolphins call him further and further out. The

Prince swims until he can swim no more. He floats on his back and looks up at the sky. The moon is full and very bright.

Slight pause.

Stacey   So ... the Prince kills himself. Is that it?

Link   Yeah.

Wayne   And that's ... the end?

Nina   Yes.

Stacey   Well, I don't think you'll have Walt Disney knocking at your door for that one. But very good, though. Very entertaining. Weren't it, Wayne?

Wayne   Yeah, very.

Sarah   When did this happen? I mean ... what time of year.

Zak   The middle of summer.

Sarah   Like the summer ... just gone.

Zak   Yes.

Nina   Does the Queen know of the Prince's death?

Zak   Not yet she doesn't.

Picks up his bags.

Link *and* **Zak** *head for door.*

Curtis   Zak?

Zak *looks at* **Curtis**.

Slight pause.

Zak *goes over to* **Curtis**.

Slight pause.

Zak *strokes* **Curtis**'s *cheek.*

Curtis *reaches out and touches the jacket.*

Slight pause.

Stacey   Wayne?

Wayne   Don't panic.

Zak and **Link** *leave.*

Nina   Time to go, my dearies – Alex! Your muscles up to it, my dear?

Alex   Yeah.

Nina   (*at* **Tommy**) What about you, Mr Ocean Desire? Or can I just call you … Ocean.

Tommy *looks at* **Curtis**.

Curtis *nods.*

Tommy   A pleasure.

Nina   Ooo! I feel a dance coming on.

Alex *and* **Tommy** *pick Nina up.*

Those with torches are turning them on.

Jez   (*at* **Curtis**) Bye.

Curtis *stares*.

Alex   Sarah?

Sarah   … Yeah.

Nina, **Alex**, **Tommy**, *followed by* **Jez**, *leave.*

Sarah *looks at* **Curtis**.

Slight pause.

Gavin *rushes in, breathless, holding his eye.*

Gavin   That … that bloke hit me!

Wayne   What bloke?

Gavin   In the gay-boy jacket – Aww! It's swelling!

Wayne   Help show the others out. It's dark.

Gavin   But I've only just got up here. I'm all out of puff.

Wayne   Well, you should quit bloody smoking, then, shouldn't you!

Gavin   But –

Wayne *growls at* **Gavin**.

Gavin *runs out.*

Stacey   Don't be a stranger, Sarah. Wayne's Mum's always asking after you. Isn't she Wayne?

Wayne   Always.

Sarah *leaves.*

Stacey   Oh, Curtis, my lovely, what's all this about?

Wayne   Think I know. It's that bloke.

Stacey   What one?

Wayne   The one in the jacket. He reminded you of your dead brother, didn't he?

Stacey   Oh, sweetheart! We thought you were all over that.

Wayne   We all lose people, buddy. You can't grieve *all* your life.

Stacey   It was awful what happened to Jason, sweetheart. I never had the pleasure of meeting him but, from what I hear, he was a charming young man with everything before him. But sometimes, you know, things happen for a reason. We don't know the reason. Only God knows that. Right, Wayne?

Wayne   Right, Stace.

Stacey   It's like when my sausage dog died. I loved that sausage dog. Banger its name was. And one day I looked in its little basket and Banger was as stiff as a board. I cried and cried. Dad wasn't much help. He said we should use it as a draft excluder. I got no sympathy at all. Dad wouldn't let me even bury Banger in the back garden. So I wrapped Banger in some kitchen foil and took him over to the park. They had a flower garden there and I thought it would be nice to bury Banger amongst all those daffodils. So I dug a hole and put little Banger in. I was just covering Banger up with earth when I heard the Park Keeper yelling at me. Oh, the names he called me. The language. I ran and ran. He chased me. I ran all the way to the market. I was gasping. I went into this corner shop to get a can of something. I took something out the cooler and opened it and swigged a mouthful. Ooo, it was delicious. It really was. I put my hand in my pocket and – no money! Not a penny! I glanced up at this lovely Pakistani gentleman behind the counter. But he was serving someone else. So I thought, I'll pop home and get the money and then I'll come back and pay him. I'd only taken one step out the bloody door when this lovely Pakistani gentleman rushes over and grabs me arm and accuses me of stealing. Me! Well, I start screaming and shouting and giving the lovely Pakistani gentleman a piece of my mind. And that's when this man comes out the shop next door. A white man! The man pays the lovely Pakistani gentleman the money I owe him and takes me into his own double-glazing shop. And who's in that shop answering the phone? Wayne. Cos the man who paid for my drink was none other than Mr Avalon. So you see, sweetheart, if it weren't for my dead Banger, I'd never have met Wayne.

Sarah *appears in doorway, holding a lit torch and a packet of photos and stuff.*

Sarah Oh. Sorry. I've … got something for Curtis.

Indicating photos.

Stacey We're just on our way home, sweetheart. D'you want to come back with us and – ?

Sarah I don't think so, Stacey.

Slight pause.

Curtis I'm staying here a bit longer.

Wayne Not a good idea, buddy.

Curtis   I'm not bloody going yet!

Stacey   … Let him have a last look round, Wayne. Get it out of his system.

Wayne   We're on the brink of a great political victory, buddy.

Stacey   We've all worked so hard for it.

Wayne   You more than anyone.

Stacey   We don't want anything to rock the boat, sweetheart.

Wayne   Nothing *can* rock the boat. So long as people behave themselves.

Wayne *and* **Stacey** *head for door.*

At the door, **Wayne** *stops and looks back at* **Curtis**.

Wayne   You know, buddy, sometimes we hear rumours about stuff and it … well, it confuses us. We wonder what's true, what's not true. It's happened to me. I've heard little whispers late at night. Did this happen? Did that happen? But you know what I do? I ask Dad. After all, he's there to look out for me. Right? So I ask Dad and whatever he tells me … that's the truth. Life's simpler that way.

Stacey   Wayne's dad loves you, Curtis.

Wayne   He's *our* dad. And, yes, he *does* love. We *all* love you. Love you very much. You know that. Don't you, brov?

Curtis   … Yes. I know.

Wayne *and* **Stacey** *walk out.*

Slight pause.

Sarah   Zak wanted me to give you these.

Curtis   What are they?

Sarah   Photos. Taken of … someone on a beach. Earlier this year.

Curtis   Have you … ?

Sarah   No.

Puts photos on table.

All those times we said, 'I wonder what Jason would've thought.' Remember? When I decided art school is what I'm going to aim for. And now – when the leaves are turning brown. He loved this time of year, didn't he. And remember how we said how pleased he would've been when you ... you and me ...

Gently weeps.

Curtis *steps towards her.*

Sarah   No!

Curtis *stops.*

Slight pause.

Sarah   I don't feel young at all. Do you? I feel like I've lived a million years and ... and gone through hundreds of wars and I can't tell anyone about them because when they look at me all they see is this ... young face. But it's not the face I should have. It's not my face.

Sarah *goes to leave –*

Curtis   Sarah.

Sarah *stops and looks at* **Curtis**.

Sarah   What?

Slight pause.

What do you want to *say*, Curtis?

Slight pause.

What do you want to do?

Curtis *doesn't move.*

Slight pause.

Sarah *leaves.*

Curtis *looks at the photos on the table.*

Slight pause.

Curtis *approaches table.*

Slight pause.

Curtis *picks photos up.*

Slight pause.

Curtis *opens packet of photos.*

He hesitates before looking at them.

Curtis *looks at first photo.*

The dogs start barking.

Curtis *continues looking at photos...*

The dogs bark louder and louder...

The dogs bark louder and louder...

Blackout.

Brokenville

All sorrows can be borne
if you put them in a story
or tell a story about them.

Karen Blixen

Characters

Child
Satchel
Glitter
Quiff
Bruise
Tattoo
Old Woman

Night. A ruined house.

Moonlight reveals rubble, damaged furniture etc.

*A ten-year-old boy is searching for something. His clothes –
T-shirt, jeans and trainers – show signs of whatever has gone
before. He will be known, quite simply, as* **Child***.*

Child *finds what he's after – a music box.*

He opens it: a haunting lullaby starts to play.

Child *gets into bed and tucks a blanket round him.*

He opens a book of fairytales. The pages are scorched and torn.

Child *stares as if reading, finding comfort in this instinctive ritual.*

Gradually, **Child** *drifts into sleep ...*

*A fifteen-year-old male enters, clutching a satchel and torch. He
is wearing a dishevelled school uniform. He will be referred to as*
Satchel*.*

Satchel *searches the ruined house with his torch.*

The light comes to rest on **Child***.*

Satchel *approaches* **Child** *and looks down at him as –*

*A sixteen-year-old female enters, clutching torch. She is wearing
a dress (decorated with silver sequins) and stilettos. She will be
referred to as* **Glitter***.*

Glitter   Who's there?

Satchel   Me. Who're you?

Glitter   I'm ...

Approaches **Satchel***.*

Glitter   What's *your* name?

Satchel   Forgotten.

Glitter   Me too.

Satchel   You've got glitter in your hair.

Glitter   Have I? … What's in your satchel?

Satchel   A notebook.

Glitter   Your name might be in it.

Satchel   No. Just blank pages.

Glitter *aims torch at* **Child**.

Glitter   I heard the music.

Satchel   Me too.

Glitter   Not with you, then?

Satchel   What?

Glitter   The child.

Satchel   Oh … no.

Glitter   … What happened?

Satchel   Where?

Glitter   Everywhere.

Satchel   I … I don't remember.

Glitter   What's the time?

Indicates **Satchel***'s wristwatch.*

Satchel   It's stopped. Midnight.

A seventeen-year-old male enters, clutching torch. He is well-built and wearing jeans, leather jacket and a T-shirt. He will be referred to by the style of his hair: **Quiff**.

Satchel and **Glitter**   Who's there?

Quiff *stares.*

Satchel   You can't remember your name, can you.

Quiff *goes to a puddle, looks at his reflection and combs hair.*

Glitter   Did you hear the music too?

Quiff *doesn't answer.*

Child *starts murmuring in his sleep.*

Quiff aims torch at **Child**.

He goes to **Child** *and pulls blanket off him.*

He wraps it round his own shoulders.

Glitter   (*at* **Satchel**) Should he do that? Should we stop him?

Quiff *goes to corner and starts combing his hair as –*

A sixteen-year-old female enters, clutching a torch. She is wearing a dark dress and a single earring. There's a bruise on her leg. She'll be referred to as **Bruise**.

Satchel and **Glitter**   Who's there?

Bruise   Just me – Who're you?

Satchel   I … I've got a satchel.

Glitter   There's glitter in my hair.

Bruise   Well … I've got a bruise.

Glitter   How'd that happen?

Bruise   I'm … I'm not really sure.

Aims torch at **Child**.

That music. I heard it from … wherever I was. It's … oh, what *is* it?

Glitter   Beautiful?

Bruise   No. I mean, yes. But that's not the word – A thing for children.

Satchel   Lullaby!

Bruise   Yes. Lullaby.

An eighteen-year-old male enters, holding a torch. He is stocky, with a closely shaven head, and wearing army-style trousers and shirt. A tattoo is visible on his arm. There's a bandage over his left eye. He'll be referred to as **Tattoo**.

Satchel and **Glitter**   Who's there?

Bruise   Who's that?

Tattoo   *I'll* ask the questions. Who're you?

Satchel   … I'm the one with a satchel.

Glitter   I've the one with glitter in my hair.

Tattoo   (*at* **Bruise**) You?

Glitter   She's got a bruise.

Tattoo   (*at* **Quiff**) What about you?

Quiff *doesn't answer.*

Tattoo   I'm talking to you! … Poncey hair!

Satchel   It's a quiff.

Tattoo   Hasn't he got a tongue?

Quiff   I've got a tongue.

Tattoo   Well, *use* it, then!

Glitter   (*at* **Tattoo**) What's *your* name?

Tattoo   Eh? Oh, I'm … I'm …

Glitter   You've got a tattoo.

Tattoo   … That's right.

Satchel   Hello, Tattoo.

Tattoo   Don't call me that –

Winces at pain in eye.

Bruise   Are you alright?

Tattoo   It's nothing.

Goes to puddle and bathes eye as –

Old Woman *enters, clutching torch. She is in her eighties and walks with the aid of a stick.*

Satchel and **Glitter**   Who's there?

Bruise   Who's that?

Tattoo   Identify yourself!

Old Woman   Don't get your knickers in a twist. It's an old woman. That's all – Who're you lot?

Satchel   Satchel.

Glitter   Glitter.

Bruise   Bruise.

Old Woman   (*at* **Tattoo**) You?

Tattoo   I'm … I'm Tattoo.

Indicates Quiff

He's Poncey Hair.

Quiff   I'm bloody not!

Glitter   He's called Quiff.

Old Woman   (*indicating* **Child**) What about the little one?

Satchel   Nothing to do with us.

The music box stops.

Child *wakes in panic and jumps from bed.*

Old Woman   Don't be scared

Tattoo   Shut him up.

Bruise   He can't help it.

Tattoo   I can't stand that noise. (*at* **Child**) Shut up!

Old Woman   Shouting's not going to help! And stop shining your torches at him!

Approaches **Child**.

Old Woman   I'm not going to hurt you. Shush now … Shush …

Gradually, **Old Woman** *gets closer to* **Child**.

She holds him.

Old Woman   He's petrified. And cold. Make a fire someone –
You! Tattoo! Things to burn! Chop-chop!

Tattoo   All right, all right.

Bruise   I'll help.

Tattoo *and* **Bruise** *start looking for firewood.*

Satchel   D'you know what time it is?

Glitter   D'you know what happened?

Bruise   D'you know where we are?

Old Woman   No, no, no. The time? Sometime! What happened?
Something! The place? At the moment it's a cold place –
Coldville! Ha! How's that?

Bruise *uncovers dead bird.*

Bruise   Oh, the poor thing.

Old Woman   What is it?

Bruise   It's a dead bird.

Satchel   A cockatoo!

Old Woman   Someone's pet probably.

Child *reaches out for dead bird.*

Old Woman   Give it to him.

Bruise *hesitates.*

Old Woman   Go on!

Tattoo *gives dead bird to* **Child**.

Old Woman   (*at* **Tattoo**) Fire! Chop-chop!

Tattoo   We need matches or something.

Old Woman   Here.

Gives lighter to **Tattoo**.

Tattoo *sets fire to pile of objects.*

Child *starts whimpering at firelight.*

Old Woman   It's only a little fire. To keep us warm.

Notices book of fairytales.

What's this…? Fairystories! You like fairystories, eh?

Child *calms a little.*

Old Woman   Want me to tell you one?

Child *nods.*

Old Woman *opens book and reads.*

'There was once a land called …' – Oh … the pages are burnt.

Child *begins whimpering again.*

Old Woman   Don't worry. I'll think of something.

Slight pause.

There was once a land where everything … everything was in ruins. No one knew what had caused everything to be broken. But broken it was. And this land was called …

Satchel   Brokenville?

Old Woman   Very good. And, like all fairy tale lands, Brokenville had a King and Queen. And the King – oh, he loved going off to wars. Exploding things and killing people – that was his idea of fun. The King loved war so much there was no love left in his heart for the poor Queen. So … so the Queen went to a wizard and said, 'If this goes on me and the King will never have a son and heir.' The wizard said, 'Put this in the King's hands the next time he mentions going off to war.' And he gave the Queen an egg.

Bruise   An egg?!

Old Woman   That's right. And the next time the King mentioned war to the Queen she put the egg in his hands and, before the King has a chance to say 'exploding things' or 'killing people', the egg hatched and a baby bird popped out. It had the most beautiful feathers the King had ever seen. The King said, 'I will stay in the castle and take care of the bird. I will never go off to war again.' And that's what he did. He built a gold cage for the bird and he fed it mashed worms and milk.

Bruise   And the Queen – did she get pregnant?

Old Woman   She did.

Glitter   Did she have a boy or a girl?

Bruise   A boy.

Old Woman   The King – oh, he was so pleased with the newborn Prince. He said, 'There's not time for bird with beautiful feathers now my son is born. I want to spend all my time being the best father Brokenville has ever known. And he opened the golden cage and said, 'You are free, beautiful bird!' And the bird flew away.

Satchel   Happy ever after.

Child *shakes his head.*

Old Woman   Eh? *Not* happy ever after? … No. Of *course* it's not! Let's see … I bet being locked in that golden cage had driven the bird mad. Am I right?

Child *nods.*

Old Woman   The bird flew around the Castle in a frenzy. And then … one feather …

Pulls feather from dead bird.

Goes into the open mouth of the baby Prince.

Bruise   No!

Old Woman   Yes! The feather chokes the baby … Dead! …
Happy with that?

Child *nods.*

Child *takes feather from* **Old Woman**.

Child *puts feather in fire.*

Old Woman   We should look for more things to burn – What
d'you think?

Child *nods.*

Old Woman   You! Quiff! Fire!

Quiff   Leave me alone.

Satchel   I'll do it. (at **Child**) Want to help?

Child *nods and helps.*

Satchel *gasps at something he's found.*

Old Woman   What?

Satchel   No, no, it's nothing.

Child *tries to see.*

Old Woman   Show him!

Satchel   But it's not –

Old Woman   Show him!

Satchel   It's a human tooth. Satisfied?

Child *leads* **Satchel** *to fire.*

Satchel   What does he want?

Old Woman   The story of the tooth.

Child *nods.*

Satchel   Oh! But … but I'm not sure if … if I can …

Child *starts to whimper.*

Tattoo   I don't want him crying again!

Old Women   He *won't* cry if he gets a *story*.

Tattoo   He *won't* cry if I *strangle* him!

Bruise   Don't you *dare*!

Satchel   There was once a land called Brokenville!

Old Woman   Aha! Very good … Well, go on.

Satchel   And … in this land there was a King and Queen –

Child *shakes his head.*

Old Woman   There's no King and Queen.

Satchel   Where are they, then?

Child *whispers in* **Old Woman***'s ear.*

Old Woman   Oh, that's wonderful – The Queen collects seashells. So the King has taken her to the beach.

Child *whispers in* **Old Woman***'s ear.*

Old Woman   They've left their son in charge.

Child *points at* **Quiff**.

Old Woman   Prince Quiff!

Child *claps excitedly.*

Glitter   He's a vain prince then.

Satchel   Every night the Prince would look at his reflection in the mirror.

Old Woman   And he'd kissed it.

Bruise   I bet he did.

Satchel   And he'd say, 'I am the most gorgeous person in all the land.'

Old Woman   And then, one night, the Prince kissed the mirror so hard it cracked.

Satchel   He cut his lip.

Old Woman   Did something crawl inside the cut?

Satchel   I think it may have done, yes … . A spider!

Old Woman   Very good. Then?

Satchel   It … it made the Prince very ill.

Old Woman   What were the symptoms?

Satchel   His hair started to fall out.

Glitter   Ha!

Old Woman   More and more hair fell out.

Glitter   Handfuls.

Bruise   Until he was bald.

Quiff   Bald!

Glitter *and* **Bruise** *laugh.*

Quiff   Shut up!

Old Woman   If you don't like the story, change it.

Glitter   He hasn't got the *brains* to change it.

Slight pause.

Quiff   The King and Queen – they've gone to … to – where was it again?

Satchel   Brokenville Beach.

Quiff   And the Prince – he's been left in charge?

Old Woman   The Kingdom's all yours.

Quiff   And what about the people?

Old Woman   We're all your humble subjects.

Quiff   … Shave your heads!

Glitter   What?!

Bruise   He can't do that.

Old Woman   Oh, yes, he can.

Satchel   So the humble subjects shaved their heads.

Quiff   Ha! Now the Prince is most gorgeous thing in all the land again. (*at* **Glitter**) Brains or what?

Satchel   And then Prince Quiff got thinner.

Quiff   Thinnner?

Old Woman   No muscles.

Bruise   Nothing but skin and bone.

Glitter   A walking skeleton.

Quiff   No! … I'm not doing this anymore.

Turns away.

Old Woman   (*at* **Child**) Wonder what's going to happen. Prince Quiff is obviously thinking of what to do next. He was very clever before, wasn't he? Wonder if he can do it again.

Quiff   … Stop eating!

Glitter   What?!

Quiff   Get as thin as me.

Bruise   Oh, this – it's just silly.

Old Woman   Silly or not, it's the law.

Satchel   So everyone stopped eating until they were as thin as the Prince.

Quiff   The Prince is the most gorgeous thing in all the land again.

Satchel   And then he spat out a tooth.

Holds up tooth.

Glitter   His teeth are falling out.

Bruise   Serves him right.

Quiff   Pull out your teeth!

Satchel   The Prince travelled the land looking at the piles of teeth and hair.

Quiff   I'm the most gorgeous thing in the –

Satchel   Now cough blood.

Quiff   Blood?

Satchel   Lots.

Tattoo   He's dying.

Quiff   I'm not!

Satchel   You are. It's *my* story.

Quiff   *I* can change it.

Old Woman   Not *this* bit you can't.

Tattoo   A haemorrhage like that – Fatal!

Glitter   You're dying. Goodbye.

Bruise   (*at* **Quiff**) Goodbye.

Tattoo   (*at* **Quiff**) Goodbye.

Satchel   And so the Prince lay on his bed and breathed his last –

Quiff   Kill yourselves.

Satchel   What!?

Quiff   If I'm going to die, then so is everyone else.

Glitter   No.

Bruise   You can't.

Satchel   It's not fair.

Tattoo   Rebellion!

Old Woman   What – ? Oh, yes! Rebellion in Brokenville! Come on, everyone!

Tattoo   Arm yourselves!

They pick up sticks and approach **Quiff**.

Quiff *backs away from them.*

Quiff   No! … Oh, come on … Don't do this …

Old Woman   Don't let him escape!

Tattoo   He's the people's enemy!

Satchel   We want justice!

Glitter   Let me get my hands on him!

Bruise   Tear him to pieces!

Tattoo, **Satchel**, **Glitter** *and* **Bruise** *are closing in on* **Quiff**.

Quiff   I … I don't like this! There must be another way! *Please!*

Old Woman   Wait! Perhaps he's right.

Satchel   What d'you mean?

Old Woman   There *might* be another way.

Quiff   What is it? Anything!

Old Woman   You could ask us to forgive you. (*at* **Child**) The Prince can ask us that, can't he?

Slight pause.

Child *nods.*

Old Woman   (*at* **Quiff**) Well, go on, then. Ask!

Quiff   … Please … . Everyone … . Forgive me?

Old Woman   (*at* **Child**) It's up to you. Do we tear him to pieces … or forgive?

Everyone is looking at **Child**.

Child *whispers to* **Old Woman**.

Old Woman   Tear him to pieces!

All   (*except* **Quiff** *and* **Child**) Kill! Kill! Kill! Kill! Kill!

They close in around **Quiff**.

Quiff   (*screaming*) NOOOOOOO!

Silence.

Child *claps ecstatically.*

Old Woman   You enjoyed that, didn't you.

Child *nods, then whispers in* **Old Woman***'s ear.*

Old Woman   Feed the Prince to the birds.

Child *makes squawking noises.*

Then –

They all make squawking noises.

They all flash their torchlight everywhere.

Slowly, their squawks fade away ...

Bruise   Perhaps the Prince's blood is magic.

Old Woman   Magic?

Bruise   Perhaps it ... well, perhaps it made everyone's hair grow back.

Glitter   And their teeth.

Satchel   Oh, I like that.

Old Woman   (*at* **Child**) Well?

Child *shakes his head.*

Bruise   But why?

Old Woman   He's right. You're still alive. That's enough –
Where's the tooth?

Satchel   Here.

Child *takes tooth from* **Satchel**.

He puts it on the fire, then points.

Old Woman   What?

Bruise   Something over here ...

Holds up a damaged hand-mirror.

This?

Child *nods.*

Old Woman   What is it?

Bruise   A mirror.

Old Woman   (*at* **Bruise**) You know what to do.

Slight pause.

Bruise   There was once a ...

Glitter   Princess Glitter?

Bruise   No.

Child *points at* **Tattoo**.

Old Woman   Aha! King Tattoo.

Bruise   But he was a blind king.

Tattoo   Why?

Bruise   Because you once had a Queen. And you didn't love her
enough. The Queen died of a broken heart. And, once she was
dead, you realized just how much you cared for her and ... and
you cried your eyes out!

Child *claps.*

Bruise   Every night the King walked in the garden of the Castle.

Old Woman   The garden was once the Queen's.

Satchel   The King wishes he could still see it.

Bruise   The Prince describes it to him.

Old Woman   (*at* **Quiff**) ... Describe it, then!

Quiff   Thought I was dead.

Old Woman   New story, new Prince.

Tattoo   Where's Prince Poncey Hair?

Quiff   You see what he's like!

Glitter   Why don't you both grow up.

Old Woman   (*indicating* **Child**) Do you want him crying again?

Tattoo   Alright, alright ... Where's Prince Quiff?

Quiff   What d'you want?

Tattoo   Oh, son. Am I glad to see you.

Bruise   You're blind.

Tattoo   I know that. I want you to describe the garden to me.

Quiff   Well ... there's roses. And butterflies. And ladybirds.

Bruise   There was nothing King Tattoo liked to do more than sit in his dead Queen's garden and smell the roses.

Tattoo   Very ... flowery.

Bruise   And then, one night, a Dragon flew out of the sky.

Satchel   Where'd it come from?

Old Woman   The nearby mountains.

Bruise   This was the first time the Dragon had ever flown so close to the castle. Can you guess why it's doing it now?

Child *shakes head.*

Satchel   The roses! It's smelt the roses!

Quiff   I was going to say that!

Bruise   The roses had been growing and growing. More and
more each year. And now the smell had reached the mountains.

Satchel   And there's nothing Dragons like more than to eat roses.

Bruise   That's right!

Old Woman   How's the King feel about this?

Tattoo   I'm bloody livid.

Quiff   Go to the Wizard.

Satchel   Hello, King.

Tattoo   Hello, Wizard. That Dragon's going to eat my garden. *Do*
something!

Satchel   Take my advice. Give it a corner of your garden. Grow
roses in this corner just for the Dragon. I'm sure it'll be happy to
leave the rest of your garden alone.

Tattoo   How d'you know?

Satchel   I know Dragons. They're not greedy.

Tattoo   I'm not having some overgrown lizard spoiling my view.

Bruise   You can't see it!

Tattoo   You know what I mean – Where's my son?

Quiff   Here.

Tattoo   Kill the Dragon.

Quiff   But the Wizard said –

Tattoo   No 'buts'. I'm not giving that Dragon one petal of my
garden! Chop its head off!

Bruise   So … Prince Quiff got the biggest sword he could find
and went to the mountains.

Slight pause.

Old Woman   Go on.

Bruise and **Glitter**   Chop-chop!

Quiff *picks up table leg and starts climbing a pile of rubble.*

Quiff   Dragon!

Old Woman   Louder.

Quiff   DRAGON!

Bruise   Then he saw something.

Old Woman   On top of the mountain.

Satchel   It was very large and … made of twigs.

Quiff   What is it?

Old Woman   You're the one up the mountain.

Quiff   … It's a nest.

Bruise   Anything inside?

Quiff   Eggs.

Bruise   And that's when the Dragon attacked.

Quiff   Why?

Bruise   Protecting its nest.

Quiff   I'm not hurting anything.

Satchel   The Dragon doesn't know that.

Bruise   The Prince stabbed the Dragon.

Quiff   Take that!

Bruise   The Dragon chased the Prince back down the mountain.

Quiff   You can't beat me! Look at my muscles! Look how I can jump. And spin. And kick. Kung Fu!

Glitter   Oh, get on with it.

Quiff swings table leg.

Quiff   There!

Bruise   What've you done?

Quiff   Chopped its head off.

Picks up piece of rubble.

Bruise   Take it to the King.

Quiff *drops rubble in front of* **Tattoo**.

Quiff   Look at it, Dad! Well, you can't. You're blind. But if you could you'd see the head of the scariest Dragon that ever lived. But I fought it and won. No problem! What a fight it was.

Tattoo   You did a good job, son.

Quiff   The Dragon didn't stand a chance against my muscles. I stabbed it and karate chopped it and –

Old Woman   But the Prince had to forget the Dragon.

Quiff   Why?

Glitter   Time to grow up.

Bruise   And marry.

Quiff   Marry!?

Old Woman   A Princess!

They all look at **Glitter**.

Glitter   … Me?!

Quiff   Who'd want to marry you? Not me.

Glitter   And who'd want to marry you? Not me.

Bruise   King Tattoo will decide.

Tattoo   Get hitched, you two.

Slight pause.

Glitter *takes a step towards* **Quiff**.

Old Woman   (*at* **Quiff**) And you! Come on!

Quiff *takes a step towards* **Glitter***.*

Eventually, they stand next to each other.

Satchel   The Prince and Princess are married!

Throws torn paper like confetti.

Others cheer and clap.

Old Woman   Honeymoon!

Quiff and **Glitter**   Honeymoon!?

Slight pause.

Quiff   Hello, Princess.

Glitter   Hello, Prince.

Old Woman   Kiss!

Glitter and **Quiff**   Do *what*?

Satchel   Snog time!

Quiff   But … I don't fancy her.

Glitter   And I don't fancy him.

Old Woman   It's for the story.

Quiff *and* **Glitter** *look at each other awkwardly.*

Gradually, they lean towards each other.

Just as it looks as if they might actually kiss –

Quiff   Did I tell you about the Dragon?

Glitter   Zillions of times.

Quiff   My sword went right into its eye. Yellow jelly spurted out.

Glitter   All right, all right, enough.

Quiff   I stabbed the other eye.

Glitter   How are we going to move the story forward if you keep on about the Dragon?

Bruise   The Princess was very upset. She loved the Prince very much –

Glitter   No I don't!

Bruise   And more than anything she wanted his child.

Glitter and **Quiff**   Now hang on!

Tattoo   The Kingdom needs the Prince to have son.

Old Woman   Get lovey-dovey! Chop-chop!

Slight pause.

Glitter   Prince … I love you so much and –

Quiff   I don't want a baby.

Glitter   But I love you and the King –

Quiff   I don't want a baby.

Glitter   Oh, I give up.

Tattoo   I'd go to the Wizard.

Old Woman   Good thinking.

Satchel   Wizard Satchel here.

Tattoo   The Princess loves the Prince so much but –

Quiff   I don't want a baby.

Tattoo   What can we do?

Satchel   I … I'm not sure …

Old Woman   Why don't you make a mirror, Wizard Satchel?

Bruise *gives mirror to* **Satchel**.

Satchel   A mirror! Good idea. Well … it's a magic mirror, obviously. Now … what can it do?

Tattoo   Don't you know?

Satchel   Not yet I don't, no.

Slight pause.

Got it! Take this mirror to Prince Quiff. When he looks in it he will see wonderful things and he'll forget all about the Dragon.

Gives mirror to **Tattoo***.*

Tattoo   So … he has to look into the mirror *all* the time?

Old Woman   … What Wizard Satchel is trying to say is … When the Prince looks into the mirror he will be so amazed by what he sees he won't be able to look away. But then you must break off tiny bits of the mirror –

Satchel   Break off tiny bits of the mirror –

Old Woman   So small the Prince won't see –

Satchel   So small the Prince won't see –

Old Woman   Until *all* the mirror is gone. By *that* time the Prince will have forgotten –

Satchel   He'd've forgotten all about the Dragon. And everything will be back to normal – How's that?

Tattoo   It'll do.

Satchel   One more thing. The mirror can be a dangerous magic. Don't look into it yourself.

Tattoo   I can't. I'm blind.

Satchel   Then there's no problem.

Bruise   So the King took the mirror to the Prince.

Hands mirror to **Quiff***.*

Quiff *looks in mirror and –*

Quiff   Wonderful things!

Satchel   What about your battle with the Dragon?

Quiff   Who cares?

Child *claps.*

Bruise   The King went to the Princess and told her about the magic mirror.

Tattoo   All we've got to do is break off little bits when the Prince is not looking. Soon there'll be no mirror. The Prince will be free of dragon memories and you and he will have that baby.

Bruise   You've not told her something you should have.

Tattoo   What?

Child *whispers in* **Old Woman**'s *ear.*

Old Woman   Good boy. Not to look in the mirror.

Bruise   So that night Princess Glitter broke a tiny piece from the mirror as she'd been told. But then she …

Glitter *looks into mirror.*

Glitter   Wonderful things!

Bruise   And then – a noise in the sky!

Tattoo   What's going on now?

Old Woman   A Dragon!

Bruise   More than one. Because, when the Prince had returned from killing the Dragon, he forgot about something.

Quiff   The eggs!

Bruise   And now these eggs have hatched and grown into big Dragons and …

Child *sniffs loudly.*

Bruise   They smell the roses.

Child *flaps arms as if flying.*

Bruise   They're coming to eat the garden.

Old Woman   Well done.

Bruise   The Dragons are coming!

Old Woman   The Dragons are coming!

Child *runs around flapping arms.*

Tattoo   Prince! Son! *Do* something!

Quiff   Wonderful things!

Tattoo   Princess?

Glitter   Wonderful things!

Tattoo   Oh, stop looking in that bloody mirror!

Satchel   I warned you!

Bruise   Before long there was no garden left. The Dragons … oh, they ate every single rose.

Child *whispers in* **Bruise***'s ear.*

Bruise   And more?

Child *points at* **Satchel***.*

Bruise   They ate Wizard Satchel?!

Quiff   Ha! Bad luck, Satch.

Child *points at* **Glitter***.*

Bruise   They ate Princess Glitter.

Quiff   Ha!

Child *points at* **Quiff***.*

Bruise   They ate Prince Quiff.

Quiff   I'm dead again.

Tattoo   Am I dead too?

Child *whispers in* **Bruise***'s ear.*

Bruise   The King lives on. He tells everyone the story. How he once had the most beautiful garden in the kingdom. And lost it. Because he wouldn't share a single petal.

Old Woman   Who's got the mirror?

Glitter *holds up mirror.*

Old Woman   You know what to do.

Glitter *puts mirror on fire.*

Child *points at* **Bruise**.

Old Woman   But … she's just told a story.

Child *touches* **Bruise**'s *earring.*

Old Woman   He wants your earring.

Bruise *gives earring to* **Child**.

Child *takes earring to* **Tattoo**.

He grabs **Tattoo**'s *hand and leads him to fire.*

Everyone gathers round.

The stories are becoming increasingly like pieces of theatre.

An ever-more inventive use of objects in house as props etc.

Tattoo   There was once a … Queen.

Bruise   Queen Bruise.

Tattoo   She lived with her son.

Quiff   Prince Quiff.

Tattoo   And they lived in a Castle. But this Castle … oh, it was very special.

Glitter and **Satchel**   How?

Tattoo   It … it was made of gold.

Holds up earring.

Glitter and **Satchel**   Why?

Bruise   I made it that way.

Quiff   What for?

Bruise   For *you*, of course. When you were born – oh, I was so happy. I wanted to keep you with me forever. Safe. So I created this Castle of Treasure. Look at it! The walls are decorated with gold leaf. Images of trees with leaves made of emeralds. Apples made of rubies. You see? Across the ceiling a map of the heavens. A million diamonds make up the Milky Way. The moon is purest silver with craters of mother of pearl. The rising sun a swirling mix of gold and platinum. And across the floor … a river made of crushed sapphires. The ripples are rarest crystal. See?

Quiff   It's amazing.

Bruise   Oh, let it amaze. Amaze so much you never want to leave. Look! The windows are made of the thickest stained glass so you can never see outside.

Quiff   Never see outside?!

Bruise   Why would you want to? All you'll ever need is here. You are cared for like no other. Your clothes are silk and stitched together with hair from unicorns.

Quiff   But …

Bruise   Oh, let me massage your temples with this perfume. It takes a million crushed roses to produce one drop … Happy?

Quiff   Happy.

Bruise   And you'll always stay with me?

Quiff   Always.

Slight pause.

What happened to Dad?

Bruise   Wh-what?

Quiff   The King. What happened to him?

Bruise   Oh … I've told you that story a million times.

Quiff   Tell me again.

Bruise   Well … A long time ago – before you were born – I wanted to go to the seaside.

Quiff   Brokenville Beach? I've heard that's quite a journey.

Bruise   It's on the other side of the Kingdom. But it has the most precious blue coral.

Quiff   So the King took you there?

Bruise   Yes. But we didn't get very far.

Quiff   What happened?

Bruise   We got lost in the Forest outside.

Quiff   Aha! So it's a *Forest* outside the castle?

Bruise   … Yes.

Quiff   What's it like?

Bruise   A terrible place.

Quiff   Have the trees got emerald leaves and ruby apples?

Bruise   Oh, no. Real trees are ugly. They don't sparkle at all. And for seven days and nights the King and me – we stumbled round these ugly, unsparkling trees. We had no idea where we were going. The King got so hungry he picked mushrooms and ate them raw.

Quiff   Didn't it make the King ill?

Bruise   In a way. He started to hear a voice.

Quiff   What voice?

Bruise   A woman. Or so he said.

Quiff   *You* couldn't hear it?

Bruise   'You're imaging things,' I told the King. 'I'm not,' said the King. 'The voice wants me to join her in her hut in the Forest.' 'Then it's a Witch,' I told him. 'Cover your ears!'

Quiff   Did he?

Bruise   Course not. The next day, I fainted with hunger and exhaustion. When I came round the King had gone. I searched and searched the Forest. And then – quite by accident – I saw the Castle. What luck!

Quiff   And the King was never found?

Bruise   His body was. Birds had pecked out his eyes.

Quiff   And – don't tell me – you were pregnant.

Bruise   It must've happened on that last night I was with the King. I thought, Well, I will *not* lose my child to the Forest like I lost my husband. So I transformed the Castle into what you see now – This wonder! All the treasure in Brokenville went into its making. Just for you.

Quiff   What a perfect mother you are.

Bruise   And what a perfect son you are.

They embrace.

Quiff   … Can I see the Forest?

Bruise   What?! After all I've just said.

Quiff   Just *once*?

Bruise   *No*!

Tattoo   But the Prince wanted to see the Forest more than anything. He searched for gaps in stained-glass windows.

Quiff   None!

Tattoo   So he decided to make one.

Quiff *picks up a spoon.*

Tattoo   He stole a platinum spoon from the dinner table. That night, when the rest of the Castle was sleeping, he went to the stained glass window and –

Quiff   I break it!

Glitter   You'll wake the Queen.

Old Woman   You'll have to grind away the glass.

Quiff   That'll take forever.

Tattoo   For nine years the Prince grinds and grinds at a small area of glass – no bigger than a thumbprint – until a hole appears.

Quiff   At last!

Tattoo   He looks through it.

Quiff   … Darkness.

Satchel   You'll have to wait till morning.

Quiff   Something's crawling through the hole.

Glitter   A spider!

Quiff   Look at it go!

Satchel   The spider goes to the Queen.

Bruise   Ouch!

Quiff   What's happened?

Bruise   The spider's bit me.

Glitter   It's poisonous.

Quiff   You look ill.

Bruise   I do?

Old Woman   Very.

Bruise   (*at* **Quiff**) Don't go to the Forest.

Satchel   The Queen's getting sicker by the second.

Bruise   Don't go to the Forest.

Glitter   Her muscles are stiffening.

Bruise   Don't go to the –

Old Woman   She's frozen!

Bruise *freezes.*

Child claps.

Quiff   Open the gates!

Takes a step through hole in wall.

I'm in the Forest. It's wonderful.

Tattoo   He found a dead blackbird.

Quiff   Wonderful!

Glitter   A twig.

Quiff   Wonderful!

Tattoo   And he took all these wonderful things back to the Castle.

Quiff *comes back into building.*

Quiff   Look, everyone. The Queen said it was a terrible place outside. But it's not. It's full of treasure. I'm going to eat squirrels and mushrooms. Drink rainwater. I want a cloak made out of … dead birds. A crown made out of twigs. And I want leaves in my hair and my skin covered with dirt.

Bruise   Where's my son?

Tattoo   Then – to everyone's surprise – the Queen woke up.

Bruise   I'm better now. Prince Quiff! Son!

Quiff *approaches* **Bruise**.

Satchel   He wore a cloak of dead birds.

Glitter   Crown of twigs.

Tattoo   Dirt on his skin.

Bruise   NOOOOOOO!

Child *laughs.*

Tattoo   That night the Queen went to –

Satchel   Me again!

Bruise   My son is –

Satchel   Bonkers!

Bruise   What can I do, Wizard?

Satchel   Whatever made him bonkers must be destroyed.

Bruise   … The Forest?

Satchel   Exactly!

Bruise   But how?

Satchel   Up to you.

Child *points at fire.*

Bruise   Burn it?

Child *nods.*

Old Woman   (*at* **Bruise**) Do it!

Bruise *takes burning stick from fire.*

She's about to throw it when –

Child *takes stick from her.*

Bruise   Wh-what's going on?

Child *gives stick to* **Quiff**.

Quiff   Me?

Old Woman   Oh, very good.

Quiff   But I love the Forest.

Satchel   That's why.

Quiff   But … but I'm not hurting anyone when I go there.

Bruise   You're hurting *me*.

Quiff   How?

Bruise   Look at you! Dirty skin. This is not the son I want.

Quiff   It's the me *I* want!

Bruise   If you don't burn the Forest – I'll … I'll kill myself! I'll find a nest of spiders and I'll lay in it until I'm bitten all over.

Quiff   Don't! *Please!*

Bruise   Then you know what to do.

Slight pause.

Quiff *goes to window.*

Quiff   Goodbye, wonderful forest.

Throws burning stick out of window.

Tattoo   A tree catches fire.

Quiff   Nooooo!

Satchel   Another tree!

Glitter   Another!

Bruise   Another!

Old Woman   Another! Another!

Tattoo   Until the whole Forest is burning! Burning!

The sun is now rising.

Glitter   Look at the sky!

Bruise   It's so red!

Old Woman   Red with fire!

Child *is becoming increasingly restless.*

He whispers in **Tattoo***'s ear.*

Tattoo   The air's full of sparks.

Bruise   So … what next?

Child *rushes to* **Bruise** *and whispers.*

Bruise   The Castle is burning.

Quiff   We can run away.

Child *rushes to* **Quiff** *and whispers.*

Quiff   My clothes are burning!

Child – *ever more frantic – whispers to* **Bruise**.

Bruise   Mine too!

Quiff and **Bruise**   Help!

Child *whispers in* **Old Woman**'*s ear.*

Old Woman   Your skin is burning.

Bruise and **Quiff**   No!

Child *is becoming hysterical now.*

Old Woman   Shush! Calm down.

Old Woman *holds* **Child**.

Gradually, **Child** *calms.*

Long pause.

Old Woman   (*at* **Child**) Is this your house?

Child *nods.*

Quiff   What happened to your family?

Old Woman   What happened to *your*s? Or yours? Can *any* of
you remember?

Child *whispers in* **Old Woman**'*s ear.*

Old Woman   He says … in the last story … perhaps not
everything was burnt …

Child whispers in **Old Woman**'*s ear.*

Old Woman   A leaf survived.

Bruise   Just … a leaf?

Glitter   And that's the end?

Old Woman   No. It's the beginning.

Child *takes earring from* **Tattoo** *and puts it on the fire.*

Old Woman   Next story, someone.

Glitter *breathes into her hands.*

Glitter   A breath. How's that?

Child *nods enthusiastically.*

Old Woman   Well, I can't wait for this one.

Glitter   In the Forest lives an ugly Witch.

Everyone looks at **Old Woman**.

Old Woman   Typical.

Quiff *laughs.*

Glitter   And this ugly Witch fell in love with a Prince.

Quiff *stops laughing.*

Glitter   Every day the witch goes to the Prince and says –

Old Woman   I've got a beautiful little hut in the Forest. You'd like it if you gave it a chance. I'll cook you my speciality. Squirrel and mushroom pie. Come on. Kiss me!

Approaches **Quiff**.

Quiff *squeals and runs.*

Others laugh.

Quiff   Shut it, you lot!

Glitter   The Prince goes to King Tattoo and tells him about the witch.

Quiff   She's rampant.

Tattoo   Oh, I remember her from years ago. In those days she used to live here.

Quiff   In the Castle?

Tattoo   She used to do magic to entertain us.

Quiff   What happened?

Tattoo   One day the land was invaded. I begged the witch to make me a very powerful weapon.

Quiff   What did she say?

Old Woman   I'm a good Witch. My magic must not be used to hurt.

Quiff   Did the enemy have very powerful weapons?

Tattoo   Very. They could destroy whole villages.

Quiff   But surely … once the Witch saw all that she must've changed her mind.

Old Woman   I'm a good Witch. My magic must not be used to hurt.

Quiff   So the war dragged on?

Tattoo   For years and years.

Quiff   We won though?

Tattoo   Eventually. But … oh, so many big explosions. So many people killed.

Quiff   Hope you taught the Witch a lesson.

Tattoo   I banished her.

Quiff   That all?

Tattoo   She would've cursed me if I killed her. (*at* **Old Woman**) You'll stay in the Forest from now on.

Old Woman *moves away.*

Quiff   And stay there, you old bag.

Old Woman   Don't you *dare* call me that … You know I love you, gorgeous Quiffy. Come here … Please.

Quiff *joins* **Old Woman**.

Old Woman   I can't sleep for thinking about you. You haunt me, you sexy thing. Please … let me touch your gorgeous skin with my finger.

Quiff   No way.

Old Woman   Then … oh, I've got it! Yes! Let me hold my hand in front of your lips and feel your breath.

Quiff   No!

Glitter   And then, one day, the land is invaded again …

Tattoo   Bid explosions! People killed!

Quiff   What can we do?

Tattoo   No idea.

Slight pause.

Quiff   Got it!

Goes to **Old Woman**.

Listen, Witchy, if I let you hold your hand in front of my mouth like you wanted … will you make me a very powerful weapon?

Old Woman   I'm a good Witch. My magic must not be used to hurt.

Quiff *turns to leave.*

Old Woman   Wait! Let me feel!

Quiff   And I'll get a weapon?

Old Woman   Yes, yes.

Feels **Quiff***'s breath and lets out an ecstatic cry.*

Glitter   And so … the Witch made the weapon.

Quiff   Big explosions! People killed!

Tattoo   But the enemy keeps on fighting.

Quiff   How come?

Tattoo   Their weapons are even more powerful. What can we do?

Slight pause.

Quiff goes to **Old Woman**.

Quiff   Hey! Witchy! If I let you … touch my hair, will you make me an even more powerful weapon?

Old Woman   I'm a good Witch. My magic must not be –

Quiff *turns to leave.*

Old Woman   No! Wait! I'll do it! Just … oh, let me touch your gorgeous hair.

Quiff   Don't mess it though.

Old Woman *strokes hair and lets out an ecstatic cry.*

Glitter   The weapon is made.

Quiff   King! Dad! Look! Explosions like you've never seen. Boom!

Tattoo   Very impressive.

Glitter   But the enemy's weapons are still stronger.

Quiff   No way.

Tattoo   Afraid so … What can we do? Any ideas?

Quiff   … Bloody hell!

Goes to **Old Woman**.

If I let you touch my finger –

Old Woman   Deal!

Grabs **Quiff**'s *finger.*

Tattoo   Victory!

Quiff   Not yet.

Tattoo   What d'you mean?

Quiff   Why don't I go back to the Witch … and ask her to make The Most Powerful Weapon of All.

Tattoo   The Most Powerful Weapon of All?

Quiff   No one will ever invade us again. They wouldn't dare.

Tattoo   Good idea. But will she do it?

Quiff   She's under my spell. She won't be able to say no.

Quiff *goes to* **Old Woman**.

Old Woman   I'm surprised to see *you* again.

Quiff   If I let you feel my skin, will you make me The Most Powerful Weapon of All?

Old Woman   The Most Powerful Weapon of All? For feeling your skin? No … I can't. The price is too high.

Turns to leave.

Quiff   Wait! I'll let you touch me … anywhere.

Old Woman   … Anywhere?

Slight pause.

No, no. I can't.

Turns to leave.

Quiff   I'll let you … hold me in your arms.

Slight pause.

I'll let you … kiss me.

Old Woman   I … no, no. I can't.

Turns to leave.

Quiff   I'll take my clothes off. Show you all my muscles. I'll stay the night with you in your hut. And you can do anything you like to me.

Old Woman   Anything?

Quiff   Anything.

Old Woman   Get in that hut!

Slight pause.

Glitter   In the morning … the Witch had changed. She was no longer old and ugly.

Quiff   You're gorgeous too.

Old Woman and **Glitter**   I know.

Old Woman *smiles and nods a*t **Glitter**.

Glitter   The way I used to look – that was a curse. All I needed was for someone to … love me.

Quiff   I … I still need The Most Powerful Weapon of All, you know.

Glitter   Of course. But … well, making it will take a little time. And be a bit painful. For me. So … until it's made you've got to stay with me in the Forest. Deal?

Quiff   Deal.

Glitter *holds hand out to* **Quiff**.

Slowly – oh, so slowly – he takes it.

They begin strolling around.

The sun is now rising.

Glitter   It's morning. My favourite time. All the little birds in the trees. All the flowers … Fancy some breakfast?

Quiff   Mushroom pie?

Glitter   With squirrel.

Quiff   Not hungry.

Glitter   … I like your hair.

Quiff Really?

Glitter Suits you.

Quiff Thanks. I … I like your hair too.

Glitter Really?

Quiff And your eyes.

Glitter My eyes?

Quiff They're … shiny. And – look! I can see me in them.

Quiff *and* **Glitter** *are face to face now, very close.*

Perhaps they might kiss …

Then –

Glitter Oww!

Quiff What's wrong?

Glitter A pain.

Quiff Where?

Glitter Belly.

Quiff What can I do?

Glitter Help me lie down.

Quiff *helps* **Glitter** *to the ground.*

Quiff Help! Someone!

Glitter Don't worry. It's only – Ahhh!

Quiff Anyone!

Glitter Look between my legs.

Quiff Do *what*?

Bruise She's giving birth!

Quiff A baby!

Glitter   A boy.

Quiff   My son.

Glitter   Take him to the river.

Quiff   He can't swim yet.

Bruise   To *wash* him.

Quiff   Oh, yeah. Of course.

Goes to puddle.

Get you good and clean, little baby.

As **Quiff** *bathes imaginary baby, something changes in him.*

He calms, becomes thoughtful.

Glitter   What's wrong?

Quiff   Oh … nothing.

Glitter   Look at his little fingers.

Quiff   … They're wonderful.

Bruise   There's a birthmark on his leg.

Glitter   Don't let anyone hurt him.

Quiff   I won't.

Glitter   You promise?

Quiff   I promise.

Glitter   Now take it to the King – this baby.

Bruise   Your child.

Old Woman   And tell him – at last – we have made it.

Quiff   What?

Glitter and **Old Woman**   The Most Powerful Weapon of All.

Child *claps with delight and lifts a shell into the air.*

Satchel   A shell!

Old Woman   (*at* **Quiff**) Quickly!

Glitter   I'm a gorgeous Princess!

Quiff   Hello, gorgeous Princess.

A fluidity and exhilarating speed to the storytelling now.

Movement, use of found objects – everything used to maximum effect.

The evolution from static narration to full-blown theatre is complete.

Glitter   Every morning I look at my refection and kiss it.

Quiff   Looks are not *everything*, you know.

Glitter   You're a fine one to talk!

Quiff   I've grown up now.

Glitter   Ha!

Quiff   I *have*.

Glitter   So … you have no interest in how gorgeous I am at all, right?

Quiff   None whatsoever.

Glitter   You sure?

Approaches **Quiff** *seductively.*

Glitter   You don't want to touch my gorgeous skin … here? Or … here? You don't want to kiss me … here? Or … here?

Quiff *goes to kiss* **Glitter** –

Glitter   Hang on! We're brother and sister.

Quiff   Brother and sist – ? Oh, don't play games.

Bruise   Don't let her annoy you, son.

Quiff   She keeps teasing me.

Bruise   Your sister teases everyone.

Glitter   No, I don't.

Tattoo   The Princess is pure as pure can be.

Glitter   You see?

Bruise   Just because you've got this old idiot wrapped round your little finger, don't mean you can fool me. You've been greedy and selfish since the day you were born. You won't be satisfied till you own the Kingdom and everything in it.

Glitter   I think Mum's getting a bit hysterical.

Tattoo   (*at* **Bruise**) It's not good for your blood pressure, you know.

Glitter   Don't want you having a stroke on us.

Quiff   They're right. You should calm down.

Bruise   I *am* bloody calm.

Quiff   I'll get you a shell!

Bruise   A shell?

Quiff   A new addition to you collection. It always relaxes you.

Bruise   My shell collection! Of course! Thank you – Hang on! I thought Brokenville beach was supposed to be on the other side of the Kingdom.

Quiff   No, no, don't you remember? Our Castle's on the cliff right beside it.

Glitter   I think she's going senile.

Bruise   A shell! Quick!

Quiff *searches near puddle.*

Glitter *hovers nearby, watching.*

Quiff   I want to find her a big pink conch.

Glitter   Do you think there's a care home for bonkers royalty?

Quiff   The Queen's not bonkers – Hey!

Points.

You see that?

Glitter   … What?

Quiff   A whale!

Glitter   Boring.

Quiff   It's not.

Glitter   Tell me *one* interesting thing about a whale.

Quiff   … They're big.

Glitter   Something else.

Quiff   … Wizard Satchel knows something else.

Satchel   I do?

Glitter   I'm waiting.

Satchel   Er … I know! How the first whale was made! Ready?

All   (*except* **Child**) Ready!

Satchel   A long time ago there were lots and lots of Wizards. One day, just to pass the time, all these wizards got together and decided to have a game. A sort of contest. To see who could change themselves into the most spectacular creature. Lots and lots of creatures were created that day.

Quiff   Like what?

Satchel   Creatures with two beaks and a hundred legs. Creatures with … horns that glowed in the dark. There was even a giant, flying seahorse.

Quiff   Where're they now?

Satchel   Don't exist.

Quiff   Why?

Satchel   As soon as a Wizard turned himself into one of these remarkable creatures he had to turn himself back again.

Quiff   Why?

Satchel   He might enjoy being this new creature so much he'll forget he was ever a Wizard. And then, one day, a wizard turned himself into a very big creature that swam in the sea.

Quiff   A whale!

Satchel   All the other Wizards cheered and clapped. They'd never seen such a remarkable creature. A few of them got carried away and turned themselves into whales too. They swam and splashed in the sea. They dived down to shipwrecks. Then they swam up, faster and faster, until – whoosh! They shot out of the ocean. Then they crashed back down – splasshhh! – sending waves all over the place. They enjoyed themselves so much they forgot they'd ever been wizards at all.

Quiff   That's a wonderful story.

Glitter   I thought it was boring.

Satchel   Boring!?

Quiff   I'm going to skim stones now.

Glitter   What?

Quiff   Skim stones across the ocean. Look! Watch this one bounce! One! Two! Three! Four! Nearly reached that bit of blue coral. That's my ambition, you know. To reach blue coral – Watch me, Princess! You see that!

Glitter   I'm going back to the Castle now.

Quiff   Don't go! Princess!

Glitter   Hear the Prince, Dad?

Tattoo   What's he getting excited about?

Glitter   He wants to kiss me?

Tattoo   He's an affectionate brother.

Glitter   He don't want *that* sort of kiss.

Tattoo   What d'you mean?

Glitter   Oh, not now, Dad. Running away from the Prince has tired me out.

Tattoo   Running away?

Glitter   I'm going to my room.

Sits on bed.

Prince Quiff!

Quiff   You called?

Glitter   Did you hit it?

Quiff   The blue coral? Not quite. But I'll get one day. And when I do – oh, we'll have a big party to celebrate. A barbeque on the beach. Everyone will be invited. All our humble subjects. And they're be music. And lots of dancing.

Glitter   And they'll be a big bowl of … what's that party drink?

Quiff   Punch.

Glitter   That's it. It'll be bright pink. And … and it'll have bits of fruit in it. Grapes and mandarin. And I'll be wearing a new dress. Dad – he bought it for me. It's all sparkling and I feel like … like …

Quiff   The Princess that you are.

Slight pause.

Glitter *looks away.*

Quiff   What's wrong?

Glitter   Nothing.

Quiff   There *is*. You're crying. Why?

Glitter   It's … oh, it's hard to … to put it into words.

Quiff   Try … Please.

Glitter   Well … it's just that sometimes … sometimes I feel like I'm the wrong character in the right story.

Quiff   And sometimes the right character in the wrong story. But never –

Glitter and **Quiff**   The right character in the right story.

They lean close to each other.

Quiff   I had a dream once. Everything was in ruins. I lost people. But you know what scared me most? I didn't cry. I didn't feel … anything.

Glitter   But you feel something now?

Quiff   … Yes.

They lean closer.

Closer …

Then –

Tattoo   You're brother and sister, don't forget.

Glitter   He … he forced his way into my bedroom.

Quiff   (*at* **Glitter**) You *called* me here.

Glitter   I did not!

Tattoo   I've had enough of you pestering your sister.

Quiff   Pestering!

Glitter   Banish him!

Tattoo   I will!

Glitter   Go on, then.

Tattoo   You're banished!

Quiff   Mum!

Bruise   What's going on?

Glitter   The King's banished the Prince.

Bruise   He can't do that.

Tattoo   I've already done it!

Glitter   And if you don't like it, he'll banish you too.

Bruise   He wouldn't dare.

Glitter   Dad?

Tattoo   (*at* **Bruise**) You're banished!

Bruise   Goodbye, then.

Glitter   Goodbye.

Quiff   Goodbye.

Glitter   Goodbye.

Bruise *and* **Quiff** *walk a bit further away.*

Glitter   Keep going.

Bruise and **Quiff** walk outside the building.

Glitter   Help me put this shark tooth necklace on, Dad.

Picks up piece of string and hands it to **Tattoo**.

Tattoo *ties it round her neck.*

Glitter   How'd I look?

Tattoo   Very gorgeous.

Bruise   You're her *Dad*, don't forget.

Glitter   Can I have all Mum's jewellery?

Tattoo   Of course you can.

Glitter   And all my brother's weapons?

Tattoo   Anything you want.

Glitter   Anything?

Tattoo   Anything.

Glitter   The sun.

Tattoo   Eh?

Glitter   Well, just a piece of it. I'm not greedy. A sunbeam. Get me one.

Tattoo   How am I supposed to do that?

Glitter   Ask the Wizard.

Tattoo *approaches Satchel.*

Satchel   So you wanna catch a –

Tattoo   I haven't told you yet!

Satchel   I'm a Wizard, dickhead!

Slight pause.

I'll make you a giant flying seahorse.

Tattoo   I don't wanna bloody –

Satchel   You can ride this giant flying seahorse up to the sky. Catch a sunbeam. Then give it to Quiff.

Tattoo   It's for the Princess.

Satchel   The *Princess*! I won't do *anything* for her.

Tattoo   Why?

Satchel   She called my story boring.

Tattoo   Then you're banished.

Satchel   Goodbye.

Tattoo   Goodbye.

Slight pause.

I'll … I'll get someone else to help me – You're a Witch, right?

Old Woman   Thought everyone had forgotten about me.

Tattoo   I need a giant flying seahorse.

Old Woman   Why?

Tattoo   If you're a Witch, you should know.

Old Woman   You're right. Forget it!

Tattoo   Make it or I'll have you … fed to the piranhas.

Old Woman   All right, all right. But be careful. Catching a sunbeam is dangerous. Better men than you have been burnt to a crisp.

Tattoo   Just make it.

Old Woman   It's behind you.

Tattoo   … Where?

Old Woman   There!

Tattoo   Where?

Old Woman   There! Giant flying seahorses are invisible.

Tattoo   Princess Glitter! I'm ready to catch the sunbeam.

Glitter   Hurry up, then.

Tattoo   A kiss before I go?

Glitter   A kiss when you get back.

Tattoo   I'm sitting on the seahorse now.

Glitter   Get that sunbeam!

Child *rushes to old cardboard box.*

He takes out a mirrorball.

Light refracts everywhere.

Tattoo   Sunbeam!

Tattoo *starts chasing* **Child**.

Child *is laughing, enjoying every moment of it.*

Others laugh and cheer.

Much joy and play.

Tattoo *takes mirrorball from* **Child**.

Tattoo   I've caught it!

Glitter   Amazing!

Tattoo   Kiss?

Glitter   Later! I want to put my sunbeam in this shell.

Picks up shell.

My glowing crown!

Tattoo *clutches his chest.*

Tattoo   Aaahhh! My heart!

Glitter   Look at me wearing my crown.

Tattoo   Won't *anyone* help me?

Old Woman   They've all been banished.

Tattoo   (*at* **Old Woman**) Well, *you* haven't!

Old Woman *helps* **Tattoo** *over to bed.*

Tattoo   Is the Princess happy?

Old Woman   Delirious.

Tattoo   That's all that matters.

Settles on bed.

Old Woman   Comfortable?

Tattoo   Not really, no.

Old Woman   Well, I can't help that.

Tattoo   I don't want to die.

Old Woman   I can't help that either.

Tattoo   I want … a kiss.

Old Woman *bends towards* **Tattoo**.

Tattoo   Not you! The Princess!

Old Woman   You! Princess!

Glitter   What?

Old Woman   Fancy kissing the King?

Glitter   No.

Old Woman   It might save him.

Glitter   I'm busy.

Old Woman   Doing what?

Glitter   Wearing the crown.

Old Woman   (*at* **Tattoo**) She won't come.

Tattoo   I only want a bloody kiss.

Old Woman   You're looking sicker by the second, I'm afraid.

Tattoo   One bloody kiss.

Old Woman   The King is dead.

Glitter   Long live the Queen!

Others   (*except* **Child**) Long live the Queen!

Child claps.

Glitter   Okay. We've got to bury the poor old King. Let's do it at sea. Could do with a boat trip. And it's such a glorious day. Come on! All aboard!

Gently sways from side to side.

Gradually, others join in.

Glitter   Look! A whale!

Satchel   It's me! Wizard Satchel! I've changed myself into a whale. Splash, splash!

Old Woman   The water's put out your sunbeam.

Glitter   My crown.

Old Woman   Now everyone can see you for what you are.

Satchel   Throw her overboard.

Old Woman   Feed her to the piranhas.

Old Woman *and* **Satchel** *are closing in on* **Glitter**.

Others (*except* **Child**) *join in.*

Glitter   No … no …

Backs away

Others get closer.

Closer …

Closer …

Glitter   NOOO –

Child   STOP!

They all look at **Child**.

Old Woman   Stop?

Child   The story – it … it can't end like this.

Satchel   It can't?

Child *shakes his head.*

Old Woman   Then … finish it for us.

Slight pause.

Go on.

Child   The whale … it splashes the boat.

Old Woman   Okay.

Child   The shell – it rolls everywhere!

Satchel   Good.

Child   The Princess chases after it.

Glitter   Do I catch it?

Child   You fall overboard.

Glitter   I drown?

Child   No. The whale swallows you up.

Satchel   Splash, splash.

Glitter   I'm eaten alive?

Child   No. You're still alive in its belly.

Glitter   I'm in a whale's belly!

Child   You'd be more scared than that.

Glitter   I'm gonna die! Help!

Child   Are you sorry for what you did to the Prince?

Glitter   Yes.

Child   Are you sorry for what you did to the Queen?

Glitter   Yes.

Child   So they're not banished anymore?

Glitter   No.

Child   Come back, you two!

Quiff *and* **Bruise** *approach.*

Child   Now, all I need is a feather.

Old Woman   Why?

Child   To tickle the whale's nose.

Satchel   I'm gonna sneeze.

Child   Sneeze out the Princess.

Satchel   Ah-tishoo!

Glitter   I'm alive!

Child   Now kiss the King!

Slight pause.

He's not thrown overboard yet, is he?

Old Woman   No, no.

Child   (*at* **Glitter**) Then give him that bloody kiss!

Glitter *kisses* **Tattoo**.

Tattoo *sits up.*

Tattoo   I'm alive!

Old Woman (*at* **Glitter**) And now … now you have to ask everyone.

Glitter   Ask them what?

Old Woman   To forgive you, of course.

Glitter   To forgive – ? But last time … when the Prince asked …

Old Woman   Ask!

Slight pause.

Glitter   … Everyone … . Please … . Forgive me?

Everyone looks at **Child**.

Old Woman   What's it to be?

Satchel   It's up to you.

Old Woman   Do we feed her to piranhas … or forgive?

Child   … Forgive!

They all clap and cheer.

Satchel   But … wait, wait! (at **Child**) Who are you in all this?

Child   Wh-what d'you mean?

Satchel   He means, who are you in the story?

Old Woman   Exactly. I'm the Witch.

Glitter   And I'm the Princes.

Quiff   We're all *someone*.

Satchel   So who are *you*?

Child   ... I'm Billy.

Pause.

Old Woman   Well, Billy. What d'you think we should do now?

Child   I'm hungry.

Old Woman   Good thinking. Food.

Child   And thirsty.

Old Woman   Breakfast! That's what we all need!

Everyone agrees.

Satchel   There's some houses over there.

Tattoo   We'll see what we can find.

Bruise   Fresh water's the main thing.

Glitter   There might be other people.

Satchel   I'm sure there are.

Old Woman   We've got a lot to do, everyone.

Child   Chop-chop!

We watch them as they go about things.

They talk amongst themselves.

Perhaps one or two of them remember their own names.

There is much joy at each remembering.

Fade to blackout.

Philip Ridley

Philip was born in the East End of London where he still lives and works. He studied painting at St Martin's School of Art and his work has been exhibited widely throughout Europe and Japan. As well as three books for adults – and the highly acclaimed screenplay for *The Krays* (winner of the *Evening Standard* Best Film of the Year Award) – he has written twelve adult stage plays: *The Pitchfork Disney*, multi-award-winner *The Fastest Clock in the Universe*, *Ghost from a Perfect Place*, *Vincent River*, *Mercury Fur*, *Leaves of Glass*, *Piranha Heights*, *Tender Napalm* (London Fringe Best Play Award nominee), *Shivered* (OffWestEnd Best New Play Award nominee), *Dark Vanilla Jungle* (Scotsman Fringe First winner), *Radiant Vermin* and *Tonight with Donny Stixx*, plus several plays for young people: *Karamazoo*, *Fairytaleheart*, *Moonfleece* (named as one of the 50 Best Works About Cultural Diversity by the National Centre for Children's Books), *Sparkleshark* and *Brokenville* (collectively known as *The Storyteller Sequence*), and a play for the whole family, *Feathers in the Snow*.

He has also written books for children, including *Scribbleboy* (shortlisted for the Carnegie Medal), *Kasper in the Glitter* (Whitbread Prize nominee), *Mighty Fizz Chilla* (shortlisted for the Blue Peter Book of the Year Award), *ZinderZunder, Vinegar Street, Zip's Apollo* and the bestseller *Krindlekrax* (Smarties Prize and WH Smith's Mind-Boggling Books Award winner), the stage play of which – adapted by Philip himself – premiered at Birmingham Rep in 2002.

He has directed three feature films from his own screenplays: *The Reflecting Skin* (winner of eleven international awards including the George Sadoul Prize), *The Passion of Darkly Noon* (winner of Best Director at the Porto Film Festival) and *Heartless* (winner of the Silver Méliès Award for Best Fantasy Film). For the latter two, Philip co-wrote several songs, of which 'Who Will Love Me Now?' (performed by PJ Harvey) was voted BBC Radio 1's Top Film Song of 1998 and was covered by the techno-house band Sunscreem (as 'Please Save Me'), becoming a club and viral hit.

In 2010 Philip, along with songwriting collaborator Nick Bicât, formed music group Dreamskin Cradle and their first album, *Songs from Grimm*, is available on iTunes, Amazon and all major download sites. Philip is also a performance artist in his own right, and his highly charged readings of his ongoing poetry sequence *Lovesongs for Extinct Creatures* have proved increasingly popular in recent years.

In 2012 *WhatsOnStage* named him as one of the Jubilee Playwrights (sixty of the most influential British writers to have emerged in the past six decades). Philip has won both the *Evening Standard*'s Most Promising Newcomer to British Film and Most Promising Playwright Awards, the only person ever to receive both prizes.